2023

FOOTBALL LEGENDS

THIS IS A MORTIMER CHILDREN'S BOOK
Text, design and illustration
© Welbeck Children's Limited 2022
Published in 2022 by Mortimer Children's Limited
An imprint of the Welbeck Publishing Group
Based in London and Sydney
www.welbeckpublishing.com

All statistical data and player heat maps provided by Opta, under license from Stats Perform.

A catalogue record is available for this book from the British Library.

10 9 8 7 6 5 4 3 2 1
ISBN 978 1 83935 166 2

Printed and bound in Dubai
Author: David Ballheimer
Commissioning Editor: Suhel Ahmed
Design Manager: Matt Drew
Picture research: Paul Langan
Production: Arlene Alexander

All facts and stats correct as of April 2022

PICTURE CREDITS
The publishers would like to thank the following sources for their kind permission to reproduce the pictures in this book.

GETTY IMAGES: ANP Sport 14; Ruben Albarrán/Pressinphoto/Icon Sport 37; Filippo Alfero/Juventus FC 102; Eric Alonso 26; Emilio Andreoli 11, 83, 103, 106B; Gonzalo Arroyo Moreno 44, 48; Matthew Ashton/AMA 47; Marc Atkins 79; Sam Bagnall/AMA 27; Lars Baron 57; Robbie Jay Barratt/AMA 29, 55, 72, 84-85, 108T; James Baylis/AMA 80; Berengui/DeFodi Images 8; John Berry 21, 73, 90; Shaun Botterill 43; Paolo Bruno 49; Clive Brunskill 16; David S. Bustamante/Soccrates 60, 62, 81; James Chance 94; Matteo Ciambelli/NurPhoto 66; Gareth Copley 106T; Patricia de Melo Moreira/AFP 58-59; Oscar del Pozo/AFP 111T; Stuart Franklin 92; Sebastian Frej/MB Media 46; Laurence Griffiths 40, 78; Matthias Hangst 70, 76; Alexander Hassenstein 98, 109B; Mario Hommes/DeFodi Images 51, 77; Catherine Ivill 15, 52; Eddie Keogh 71; Chloe Knott 25, 42; Roland Krivec/DeFodi Images 30; Maurizio Lagana 110B; Sylvain Lefevre 24, 53; Alex Livesey 6-7, 38, 67, 91, 97; Marco Luzzani 75; MB Media 19; Manchester City FC 107B; Marcio Machado/Eurasia Sport Images 56; Giuseppe Maffia/NurPhoto 100; Angel Martinez 32-33, 68; Matt McNulty/Manchester City FC 20, 34; Aurelien Meunier/PSG 74; Alex Morton 89; Jonathan Moscrop 13, 28, 65; Alex Pantling 41; Pressinphoto/Icon Sport 45; Quality Sport Images 63, 88; Manuel Queimadelos/Quality Sport Images 23; David Ramos 96; Michael Regan 86, 107T; Alessandro Sabattini 93; Pedro Salado/Quality Sport Images 17; Fran Santiago 87; Oli Scarff/AFP 5; Lukas Schulze/Bundesliga 64; Justin Setterfield 95, 109T; Alexandre Simoes/Borussia Dortmund 18, 36; Diego Souto/Quality Sport Images 50, 99; Christof Stache/AFP 22; Simon Stacpoole/Offside 101; Boris Streubel 12; Tottenham Hotspur FC 61, 69; Cristian Trujillo/ Quality Sport Images 39; Nicolas Tucat/AFP 110T; VI Images 54; Mateo Villalba/Quality Sport Images 35, 108B; Visionhaus 9, 31, 82; Darren Walsh 10, 111B; Charlotte Wilson/Offside 104-105

FOOTBALL LEGENDS
2023

STATS • PROFILES • TOP PLAYERS

MORTIMER

CONTENTS

HOW TO USE THIS BOOK

Welcome to *Football Legends 2023* — the exciting book packed with the performance stats of the biggest stars in the world of football today! We have chosen more than 100 players and managers from the world's top five leagues: the Bundesliga in Germany, La Liga in Spain, France's Ligue 1, the Italian Serie A and the English Premier League.

You can use this book to figure out who you think the best performers are or you could even get together with friends and play a sort of trading-cards game, comparing the performance records of today's finest defenders, midfielders, forwards, goalkeepers and managers.

The types of stats featured for each position vary, as each position performs a specific role on the pitch. For example, a defender's main job is to stop the opposition from scoring, so the stats focus mainly on this part of their game. Likewise, a striker's tackling is not as relevant as their goal or assists tally. What you will find for all the players is the heat map, which shows how much of the pitch a player covers or, with goalkeepers, whether their strengths lie in the six-yard box or playing as sweeper-keepers who are comfortable all around the penalty area.

The stats span a player's career to date, playing for teams belonging to one of the top five European leagues. The figures have been collected from domestic league and European match appearances only, and exclude data from domestic cup, super cups or international games. This narrow data pool means that the information is instantly comparable so you can decide for yourself who truly deserves to be known as a living legend of the beautiful game.

DEFENDERS

There are different types of defenders. They cover a range of positions and have different skills. The centre-backs are the big defenders in the middle who mark the opposition strikers. Full-backs operate out wide: they are quick, agile and try to stop wide attackers from crossing balls into the box. Wing-backs play out wide, too, in front of the centre-backs, but also make attacking runs when they have the chance. Finally, the sweeper is the spare defender who is positioned behind the centre-half, ready to help the back four deal with any danger.

WHAT DO THESE STATS MEAN?

75%

AERIAL DUELS WON
This is the percentage of headers a defender has won in his own penalty area, to interrupt an opposition attack.

INTERCEPTIONS
This is the number of times a defender has successfully stopped an attack without needing to make a tackle.

BLOCKS
A shot that is intercepted by a defender - preventing his keeper from having to make a save - counts as a block.

KEY PASSES/PASS COMPLETION
A key pass is one that results in an attacking opportunity. Pass completion indicates as a percentage the player's passing accuracy.

CLEARANCES
An attack successfully foiled, either by kicking or heading the ball away from danger, is regarded as a clearance.

TACKLES
This is the number of times a defender has challenged and dispossessed the opposition without committing a foul.

Did you know?

For about 40 years from the late 19th century, the most common formation was 2–3–5. It featured only two defenders (right-back and left-back), while the centre-half played in midfield. There were five forwards.

NATIONALITY
Austrian

CURRENT CLUB
Real Madrid

DAVID ALABA

Although his best position is left-back, David Alaba's strength is his versatility. Superb with his positioning and reading of the game, his pace and athleticism also allow him to snuff out attacks before they have begun.

BIRTHDATE	24/06/1992
POSITION	LEFT-BACK
HEIGHT	1.80 M
WEIGHT	78 KG
PREFERRED FOOT	LEFT

BLOCKS
106

APPEARANCES
426

INTERCEPTIONS
552

AERIAL DUELS WON
48.9%

PENALTIES SCORED
3

PASS COMPLETION
89.6%

GOALS
31

KEY PASSES
380

CLEARANCES
576

TACKLES
539

MAJOR CLUB HONOURS
- ⚽ Bundesliga: 2010, 2013-2021 (B. Munich)
- ⚽ UEFA Champions League: 2013, 2020 (B. Munich)
- ⚽ FIFA Club World Cup: 2013, 2020 (B. Munich)
- ⚽ DFB-Pokal: 2013, 2014, 2016, 2019. 2020 (B.Munich)

INTERNATIONAL HONOURS
- ⚽ None to date

ACTIVITY AREAS

TRENT ALEXANDER-ARNOLD

Counted among the world's most exciting young talents, Trent Alexander-Arnold plays at right-back or right wing-back. He is fast, tackles superbly and is capable of whipping in accurate crosses that strikers love to feast on!

NATIONALITY
English

CURRENT CLUB
Liverpool

66

BIRTHDATE	07/10/1998
POSITION	FULL-BACK
HEIGHT	1.75 M
WEIGHT	69 KG
PREFERRED FOOT	RIGHT

APPEARANCES
198

BLOCKS
27

INTERCEPTIONS
260

PENALTIES SCORED
0

AERIAL DUELS WON
33.2%

PASS COMPLETION
77.1%

GOALS
11

KEY PASSES
391

CLEARANCES
317

TACKLES
327

MAJOR CLUB HONOURS
- Premier League: 2020
- UEFA Champions League: 2019
- UEFA Champions League: runner-up 2018
- FIFA Club World Cup: 2019

INTERNATIONAL HONOURS
- UEFA Nations League: third place 2019

ACTIVITY AREAS

9

28

NATIONALITY
Spanish

CURRENT CLUB
Chelsea

CÉSAR AZPILICUETA

Right-back César Azpilicueta is a natural leader, who can play anywhere on the pitch. He is excellent at using his positional sense to snuff out danger and frequently starts counter-attacks with a great right foot.

BIRTHDATE	28/08/1989
POSITION	FULL-BACK
HEIGHT	1.78 M
WEIGHT	76 KG
PREFERRED FOOT	RIGHT

APPEARANCES
550

BLOCKS
195

INTERCEPTIONS
1046

AERIAL DUELS WON
57.8%

PENALTIES SCORED
0

GOALS
14

PASS COMPLETION
84.1%

KEY PASSES
388

TACKLES
1484

CLEARANCES
1757

MAJOR CLUB HONOURS
⚽ Premier League: 2015, 2017 ⚽ UEFA Champions League: 2021 ⚽ UEFA Europa League: 2013, 2019
⚽ FIFA Club World Cup: 2021, runner-up 2012
⚽ UEFA Super Cup: 2021 ⚽ FA Cup: 2018, 2021

INTERNATIONAL HONOURS
⚽ UEFA Nations League: runner-up 2021
⚽ FIFA Confederations Cup: runner-up 2013

ACTIVITY AREAS

LEONARDO BONUCCI

Italy's vice captain Leonardo Bonucci is a strong and experienced centre-back with exceptional ball skills. He is superb at breaking up play and launching attacks with long passes. What's more, he poses a goal threat from set pieces.

NATIONALITY
Italian

CURRENT CLUB
Juventus

19

BIRTHDATE	01/05/1987
POSITION	CENTRAL
HEIGHT	1.90 M
WEIGHT	85 KG
PREFERRED FOOT	RIGHT

APPEARANCES
507

BLOCKS
319

INTERCEPTIONS
867

AERIAL DUELS WON
54.4%

PENALTIES SCORED
3

PASS COMPLETION
86.7%

GOALS
30

KEY PASSES
150

CLEARANCES
2101

TACKLES
599

MAJOR CLUB HONOURS
⚽ Serie A: 2006 (Inter Milan), 2012, 2013, 2014, 2015, 2016, 2017, 2019, 2020
⚽ Coppa Italia: 2015, 2016, 2017, 2021

INTERNATIONAL HONOURS
⚽ UEFA European Championship: 2020-runner-up 2012
⚽ FIFA Confederations Cup: third place 2013

ACTIVITY AREAS

NATIONALITY
Belgian

CURRENT CLUB
Hertha Berlin

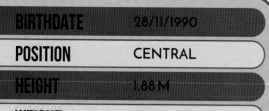

DEDRYCK BOYATA

Dedryck Boyata is equally comfortable playing at right-back or centre-half. He reads the game brilliantly and makes timely blocks and interceptions using his great positional sense before quickly distributing the ball downfield.

BIRTHDATE	28/11/1990
POSITION	CENTRAL
HEIGHT	1.88 M
WEIGHT	84 KG
PREFERRED FOOT	RIGHT

APPEARANCES
118

BLOCKS
92

INTERCEPTIONS
193

AERIAL DUELS WON
63.8%

PASS COMPLETION
87.5%

PENALTIES SCORED
0

GOALS
6

KEY PASSES
26

TACKLES
133

CLEARANCES
508

MAJOR CLUB HONOURS
- FA Cup: 2011 (Man City)
- Scottish Premiership: 2016, 2017, 2018, 2019 (Celtic)
- Scottish Cup: 2017, 2018 (Celtic)

INTERNATIONAL HONOURS
- FIFA World Cup: third place 2018

ACTIVITY AREAS

GEORGIO CHIELLINI

The Italian is a hard-tackling centre-back whose no-nonsense approach to winning the ball makes him tough to beat. He can also play as an emergency attacker and is famous for beating his chest in celebration whenever he scores.

NATIONALITY
Italian

CURRENT CLUB
Juventus

3

BIRTHDATE	14/08/1984
POSITION	CENTRAL
HEIGHT	1.87 M
WEIGHT	85 KG
PREFERRED FOOT	LEFT

APPEARANCES
512

BLOCKS
281

INTERCEPTIONS
1485

PENALTIES SCORED
0

AERIAL DUELS WON
67%

PASS COMPLETION
84.8%

GOALS
31

KEY PASSES
239

CLEARANCES
3190

TACKLES
1305

MAJOR CLUB HONOURS
⚽ Serie A: 2012-2020
⚽ UEFA Champions League: runner-up 2015, 2017
⚽ Coppa Italia: 2015, 2016, 2017, 2018, 2021

INTERNATIONAL HONOURS
⚽ UEFA European Championship: runner-up 2012, winner 2020 ⚽ FIFA Confederations Cup: third place 2013 ⚽ UEFA Nations League: third place 2021 ⚽ Olympic Games: bronze medal 2004

ACTIVITY AREAS

5

NATIONALITY
Belgian

CURRENT CLUB
Olympique Lyonnais

JASON DENAYER

A strong, intelligent central defender, Jason Denayer's excellent positional sense is matched by good tackling technique and distribution of the ball. His ability to read the game makes him an asset at the back.

BIRTHDATE	28/06/1995
POSITION	CENTRAL
HEIGHT	1.84 M
WEIGHT	76 KG
PREFERRED FOOT	RIGHT

APPEARANCES
159

INTERCEPTIONS
162

BLOCKS
139

AERIAL DUELS WON
52.3%

PASS COMPLETION
86.6%

PENALTIES SCORED
0

GOALS
6

KEY PASSES
20

TACKLES
168

CLEARANCES
536

MAJOR CLUB HONOURS
- Scottish Premiership: 2015 (Celtic)
- Turkish Süper Lig: 2016 (Galatasaray)
- Turkish Cup: 2016 (Galatasaray)

INTERNATIONAL HONOURS
- None to date

ACTIVITY AREAS

RÚBEN DIAS

Rúben Dias plays mainly on the left side of central defence, but is comfortable anywhere along the back line. He excels at winning challenges in the air and on the ground, making interceptions and delivering great passes with both feet.

NATIONALITY
Portuguese

CURRENT CLUB
Manchester City

BIRTHDATE	14/05/1997
POSITION	CENTRAL
HEIGHT	1.86 M
WEIGHT	82 KG
PREFERRED FOOT	RIGHT

APPEARANCES
95

BLOCKS
57

INTERCEPTIONS
95

AERIAL DUELS WON
57.2%

PENALTIES SCORED
0

PASS COMPLETION
91.3%

GOALS
5

KEY PASSES
25

CLEARANCES
270

TACKLES
108

MAJOR CLUB HONOURS
⚽ Premier League: 2021
⚽ UEFA Champions League: runner-up 2021
⚽ Portuguese Premier Liga: 2019 (Benfica)

INTERNATIONAL HONOURS
⚽ UEFA Nations League: 2019

ACTIVITY AREAS

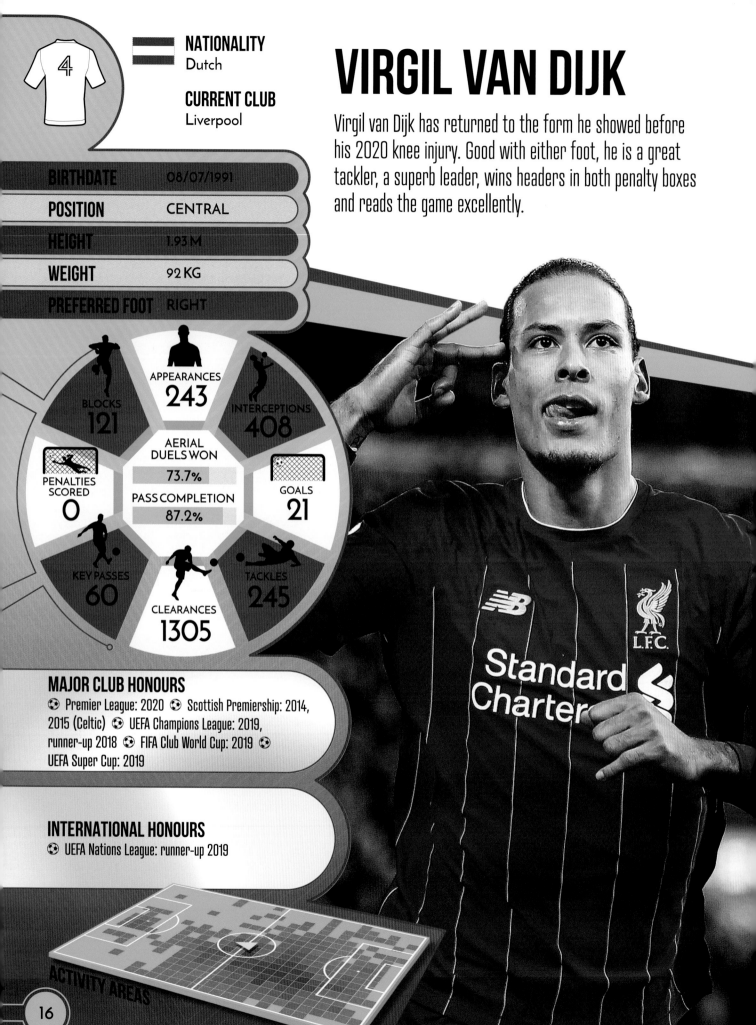

4

NATIONALITY
Dutch

CURRENT CLUB
Liverpool

VIRGIL VAN DIJK

Virgil van Dijk has returned to the form he showed before his 2020 knee injury. Good with either foot, he is a great tackler, a superb leader, wins headers in both penalty boxes and reads the game excellently.

BIRTHDATE	08/07/1991
POSITION	CENTRAL
HEIGHT	1.93 M
WEIGHT	92 KG
PREFERRED FOOT	RIGHT

APPEARANCES
243

BLOCKS
121

INTERCEPTIONS
408

AERIAL DUELS WON
73.7%

PASS COMPLETION
87.2%

PENALTIES SCORED
0

GOALS
21

KEY PASSES
60

TACKLES
245

CLEARANCES
1305

MAJOR CLUB HONOURS
⚽ Premier League: 2020 ⚽ Scottish Premiership: 2014, 2015 (Celtic) ⚽ UEFA Champions League: 2019, runner-up 2018 ⚽ FIFA Club World Cup: 2019 ⚽ UEFA Super Cup: 2019

INTERNATIONAL HONOURS
⚽ UEFA Nations League: runner-up 2019

ACTIVITY AREAS

JOSÉ GIMÉNEZ

The Uruguayan is a tough-tackling centre-back who is quick off the mark and difficult to knock off the ball. He made his international debut when he was just 19 and has also thrived at club level since joining Atlético Madrid in 2013.

NATIONALITY
Uruguayan

CURRENT CLUB
Atlético Madrid

2

BIRTHDATE	20/01/1995
POSITION	CENTRAL
HEIGHT	1.85 M
WEIGHT	80 KG
PREFERRED FOOT	RIGHT

APPEARANCES
221

INTERCEPTIONS
387

BLOCKS
134

AERIAL DUELS WON
66.2%

PASS COMPLETION
82%

GOALS
6

PENALTIES SCORED
0

KEY PASSES
107

TACKLES
340

CLEARANCES
996

MAJOR CLUB HONOURS
- ⚽ La Liga: 2014, 2021
- ⚽ UEFA Europa League: 2018
- ⚽ UEFA Super Cup: 2018
- ⚽ UEFA Champions League: runner-up 2014, 2016

INTERNATIONAL HONOURS
- ⚽ FIFA U-20 World Cup: runner-up 2013
- ⚽ China Cup: 2018, 2019

ACTIVITY AREAS

NATIONALITY
German

CURRENT CLUB
Borussia Dortmund

15

MATS HUMMELS

The German is regarded as one of the best ball-playing defenders on the planet. Hummels can physically tussle with the strongest of forwards, but it is his ability to stride forward and set up attacks with his fine passing that sets him apart.

BIRTHDATE	16/12/1988
POSITION	CENTRAL
HEIGHT	1.91 M
WEIGHT	94 KG
PREFERRED FOOT	RIGHT

BLOCKS
210

APPEARANCES
479

INTERCEPTIONS
1074

AERIAL DUELS WON
67%

PASS COMPLETION
84.2%

PENALTIES SCORED
1

GOALS
35

KEY PASSES
176

CLEARANCES
1979

TACKLES
1118

MAJOR CLUB HONOURS
⚽ Bundesliga: 2011, 2012, 2017 (B. Mun), 2018 (B. Munich), 2019 (B. Munich) ⚽ DFB-Pokal: 2012, 2019 (B. Mun), 2021
⚽ UEFA Champions League: runner-up 2013

INTERNATIONAL HONOURS
⚽ FIFA World Cup: 2014

ACTIVITY AREAS

KALIDOU KOULIBALY

Kalidou Koulibaly is an aggressive centre-back, perfect for his side's high-pressing game. Extremely fast, he is capable of sprinting back to cover even if the opposition play the ball over the top or in behind his team's high defensive line.

NATIONALITY
Senegalese

CURRENT CLUB
Napoli

26

BIRTHDATE	20/06/1991
POSITION	CENTRAL
HEIGHT	1.87 M
WEIGHT	89 KG
PREFERRED FOOT	RIGHT

APPEARANCES
305

BLOCKS
250

INTERCEPTIONS
515

AERIAL DUELS WON
55.9%

PASS COMPLETION
88.7%

PENALTIES SCORED
0

GOALS
12

KEY PASSES
84

CLEARANCES
1093

TACKLES
599

MAJOR CLUB HONOURS
⚽ Belgian Cup: 2013 (Genk)
⚽ Coppa Italia: 2020

INTERNATIONAL HONOURS
⚽ Africa Cup of Nations: 2021, runner-up 2019

ACTIVITY AREAS

14

NATIONALITY
Spanish

CURRENT CLUB
Manchester City

AYMERIC LAPORTE

Aymeric Laporte has become one of Europe's best central defenders. Very strong, he is powerful in the tackle, excellent in the air and a good organiser at the back. Laporte can also start attacks with his precise passing out of defence.

BIRTHDATE	27/05/1994
POSITION	CENTRAL
HEIGHT	1.91 M
WEIGHT	86 KG
PREFERRED FOOT	LEFT

BLOCKS
125

APPEARANCES
318

INTERCEPTIONS
627

AERIAL DUELS WON
64.9%

PENALTIES SCORED
0

PASS COMPLETION
90.1%

GOALS
16

KEY PASSES
77

CLEARANCES
1150

TACKLES
537

MAJOR CLUB HONOURS
- Premier League: 2018, 2019, 2021
- UEFA Champions League: runner-up 2021
- FA Cup: 2019

INTERNATIONAL HONOURS
- UEFA Nations League: runner-up 2021
- UEFA European U-19 Championship: runner-up 2013 (France)

ACTIVITY AREAS

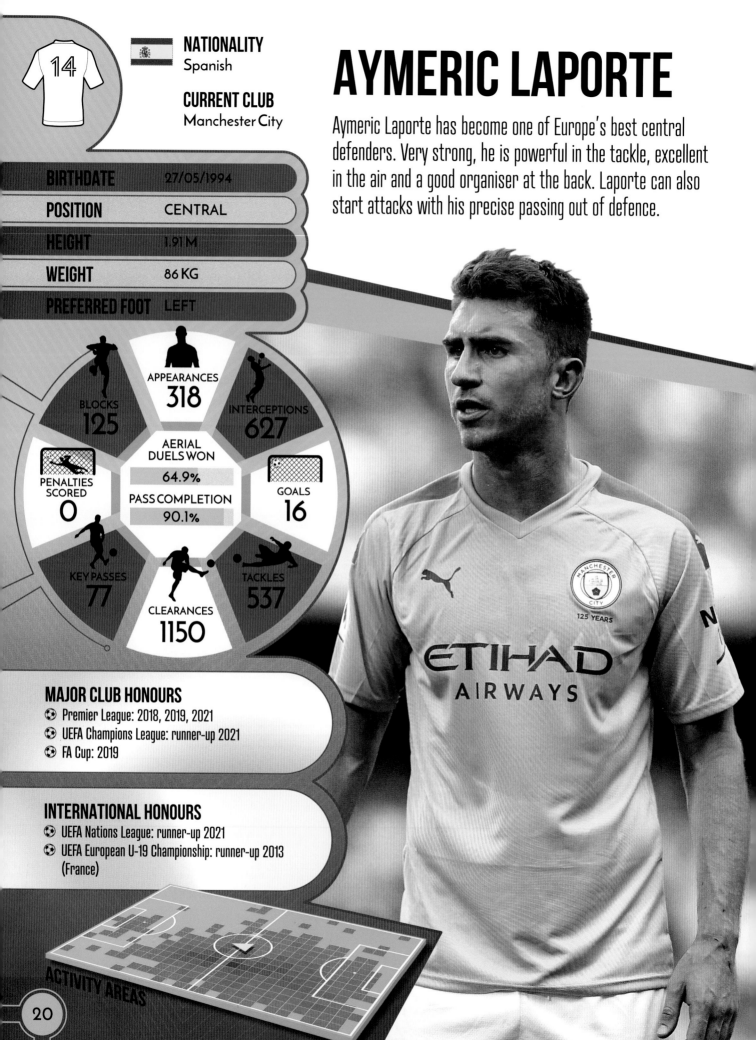

MARQUINHOS

Marquinhos is a clever defender. He may not be a powerhouse like many of today's top-class centre-backs, but has the speed, agility and intelligence to mark the quickest forwards, plus he can be very effective going forward.

NATIONALITY
Brazilian

CURRENT CLUB
Paris Saint-Germain

BIRTHDATE	14/05/1994
POSITION	CENTRAL
HEIGHT	1.83 M
WEIGHT	75 KG
PREFERRED FOOT	RIGHT

APPEARANCES
328

BLOCKS
200

INTERCEPTIONS
471

AERIAL DUELS WON
57.9%

PENALTIES SCORED
0

PASS COMPLETION
91.6%

GOALS
29

KEY PASSES
64

CLEARANCES
1179

TACKLES
528

MAJOR CLUB HONOURS
⚽ Ligue 1: 2014, 2015, 2016, 2018, 2019, 2020
⚽ UEFA Champions League: runner-up 2020
⚽ Coupe de France: 2015, 2016, 2017, 2018, 2020, 2021

INTERNATIONAL HONOURS
⚽ Copa América: 2019, runner-up 2021
⚽ Olympic Games: 2016

ACTIVITY AREAS

NATIONALITY
French

CURRENT CLUB
Bayern Munich

BENJAMIN PAVARD

One of the stars to emerge at the 2018 World Cup, Benjamin Pavard has since matured into a technically brilliant defender at Bayern Munich. He is usually in the right place at the right time to tackle or intercept dangerous passes.

BIRTHDATE	28/03/1996
POSITION	CENTRAL
HEIGHT	1.86 M
WEIGHT	76 KG
PREFERRED FOOT	RIGHT

BLOCKS 87

APPEARANCES 185

INTERCEPTIONS 336

AERIAL DUELS WON 60.4%

PASS COMPLETION 87.2%

PENALTIES SCORED 0

GOALS 5

KEY PASSES 85

CLEARANCES 581

TACKLES 239

MAJOR CLUB HONOURS
⚽ Bundesliga: 2020, 2021 ⚽ UEFA Champions League: 2020
⚽ UEFA Super Cup: 2020 ⚽ FIFA Club World Cup: 2020
⚽ DFB-Pokal: 2020

INTERNATIONAL HONOURS
⚽ FIFA World Cup: 2018
⚽ UEFA Nations League: 2021

ACTIVITY AREAS

GERARD PIQUÉ

Gerard Piqué is still classed among the best defenders in the world. Normally a centre-half, he can also play at sweeper or in front of the defence. He is an accurate passer, plus his height gives him an aerial advantage over his opponents.

 **NATIONALITY**
Spanish

CURRENT CLUB
Barcelona

 3

BIRTHDATE	02/02/1987
POSITION	CENTRAL
HEIGHT	1.94 M
WEIGHT	85 KG
PREFERRED FOOT	RIGHT

APPEARANCES
552

BLOCKS
284

INTERCEPTIONS
801

AERIAL DUELS WON
66%

PENALTIES SCORED
0

PASS COMPLETION
89.8%

GOALS
48

KEY PASSES
92

CLEARANCES
2348

TACKLES
835

MAJOR CLUB HONOURS
⚽ La Liga: 2009, 2010, 2011, 2013, 2015, 2016, 2018, 2019 ⚽ UEFA Champions League: 2008 (Man. Utd), 2009, 2011, 2015 ⚽ UEFA Super Cup: 2009, 2011, 2015 ⚽ FIFA Club World Cup: 2009, 2011, 2015

INTERNATIONAL HONOURS
⚽ FIFA World Cup: 2010
⚽ UEFA European Championship: 2012

ACTIVITY AREAS

23

4

NATIONALITY
Spanish

CURRENT CLUB
Paris Saint-Germain

SERGIO RAMOS

Very quick at anticipating danger, Sergio Ramos is a fine tackler with an excellent positional sense. Not only is he a skilled defender and great team leader, but is also known for regularly scoring important goals for his team.

BIRTHDATE	30/03/1986
POSITION	CENTRAL
HEIGHT	1.84 M
WEIGHT	82 KG
PREFERRED FOOT	RIGHT

APPEARANCES
649

INTERCEPTIONS
1433

BLOCKS
298

AERIAL DUELS WON
67.3%

PENALTIES SCORED
18

PASS COMPLETION
89.6%

GOALS
91

KEY PASSES
284

CLEARANCES
2674

TACKLES
1325

MAJOR CLUB HONOURS
La Liga: 2007, 2008, 2012, 2017, 2020 (R. Madrid)
UEFA Champions League: 2014, 2016, 2017, 2018 (R. Madrid)
UEFA Super Cup: 2014, 2016, 2017 (R. Madrid) FIFA Club World Cup: 2014, 2016, 2017, 2018 (R. Madrid)

INTERNATIONAL HONOURS
FIFA World Cup: 2010
UEFA European Championship: 2008, 2012
FIFA Confederations Cup: third place 2009, runner-up 2013

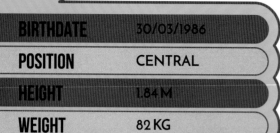

ACTIVITY AREAS

ANTONIO RÜDIGER

Antonio Rüdiger has quietly become a dominant defender all along the back line, winning tackles with his great strength and dominating the penalty area with his heading ability. He is also an excellent passer, reads the game well and leads by example.

CURRENT CLUB
Chelsea

2

BIRTHDATE	03/03/1993
POSITION	CENTRAL
HEIGHT	1.91 M
WEIGHT	81 KG
PREFERRED FOOT	RIGHT

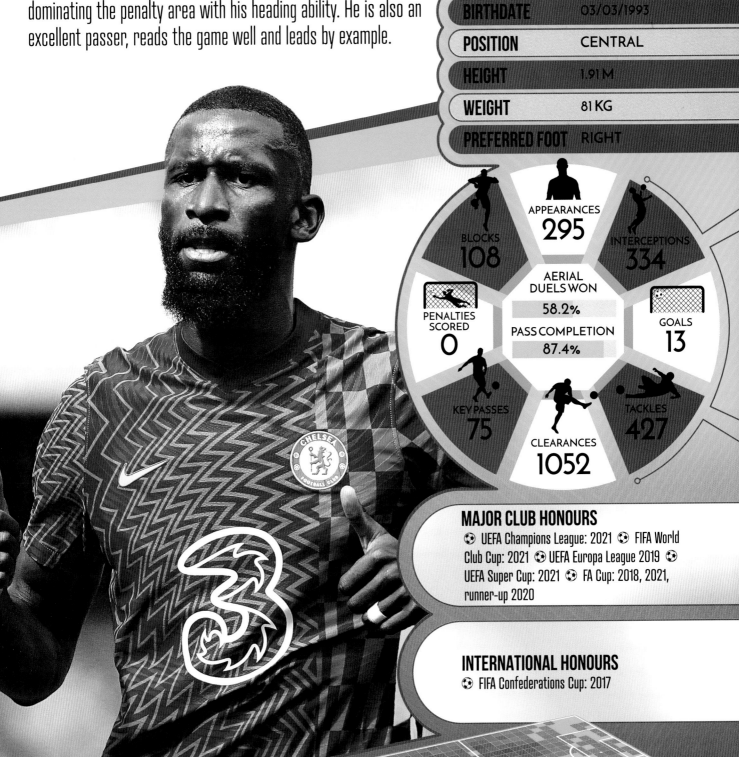

APPEARANCES
295

BLOCKS
108

INTERCEPTIONS
334

PENALTIES SCORED
0

AERIAL DUELS WON
58.2%

PASS COMPLETION
87.4%

GOALS
13

KEY PASSES
75

CLEARANCES
1052

TACKLES
427

MAJOR CLUB HONOURS
⚽ UEFA Champions League: 2021 ⚽ FIFA World Club Cup: 2021 ⚽ UEFA Europa League 2019 ⚽ UEFA Super Cup: 2021 ⚽ FA Cup: 2018, 2021, runner-up 2020

INTERNATIONAL HONOURS
⚽ FIFA Confederations Cup: 2017

ACTIVITY AREAS

25

15

NATIONALITY
Montenegran

CURRENT CLUB
Atlético Madrid

STEFAN SAVIĆ

Stefan Savic reads the game well but his biggest strength is his ability in the air. He is comfortable on the ball and neat with his short passing, relying on brains rather than brawn to operate effectively at the back.

BIRTHDATE	08/01/1991
POSITION	CENTRAL
HEIGHT	1.88 M
WEIGHT	82 KG
PREFERRED FOOT	RIGHT

APPEARANCES
324

BLOCKS
194

INTERCEPTIONS
581

AERIAL DUELS WON
63.7%

PENALTIES SCORED
0

PASS COMPLETION
83.6%

GOALS
8

KEY PASSES
40

TACKLES
416

CLEARANCES
1634

MAJOR CLUB HONOURS
- ⚽ La Liga: 2021
- ⚽ UEFA Europa League: 2018
- ⚽ UEFA Super Cup: 2018
- ⚽ Premier League: 2012 (Man City)

INTERNATIONAL HONOURS
- ⚽ None to date

ACTIVITY AREAS

THIAGO SILVA

Players past and present rate Thiago Silva as one of the best-ever central defenders to play the game. In addition to his technical strengths, he is a natural leader who is able to inspire team-mates to raise their game in the heat of battle.

NATIONALITY
Brazilian

CURRENT CLUB
Chelsea

BIRTHDATE	22/09/1984
POSITION	CENTRAL
HEIGHT	1.83 M
WEIGHT	79 KG
PREFERRED FOOT	RIGHT

APPEARANCES
441

BLOCKS
300

INTERCEPTIONS
959

AERIAL DUELS WON
72.1%

PASS COMPLETION
92.2%

PENALTIES SCORED
0

GOALS
23

KEY PASSES
99

CLEARANCES
2284

TACKLES
652

MAJOR CLUB HONOURS
- ⚽ UEFA Champions League: 2021, runner-up 2020 (PSG)
- ⚽ UEFA Super Cup: 2021 ⚽ FIFA Club World Cup: 2021
- ⚽ Serie A: 2011 (Milan) ⚽ Ligue 1: (x 7) 2013-2020 (PSG)
- ⚽ Coupe de France: 2015, 2016, 2017, 2018, 2020 (PSG)

INTERNATIONAL HONOURS
- ⚽ FIFA Confederations Cup; 2013
- ⚽ Copa América: 2019, runner-up 2021

ACTIVITY AREAS

37

NATIONALITY
Slovakian

CURRENT CLUB
Inter Milan

MILAN ŠKRINIAR

Centre-back Milan Škriniar is a forceful tackler, strong in the air and combative on the ground. But what sets Škriniar apart are his ball-playing skills and ability to stay calm under pressure and pick out intelligent passes.

BIRTHDATE	11/02/1995
POSITION	CENTRAL
HEIGHT	1.87 M
WEIGHT	80 KG
PREFERRED FOOT	LEFT

APPEARANCES
230

BLOCKS
156

INTERCEPTIONS
226

AERIAL DUELS WON
51.5%

PASS COMPLETION
91.2%

PENALTIES SCORED
0

GOALS
11

KEY PASSES
50

TACKLES
384

CLEARANCES
803

MAJOR CLUB HONOURS
⚽ Serie A: 2021
⚽ UEFA Europa League: runner-up 2020

INTERNATIONAL HONOURS
⚽ King's Cup: 2018

ACTIVITY AREAS

JOHN STONES

Currently counted among the world's best defenders, John Stones couples his comfort in possession with all the necessary technical defensive attributes. He is composed under pressure, wins headers, tackles well and is a big-match player.

NATIONALITY
English

CURRENT CLUB
Manchester City

5

BIRTHDATE	28/05/1994
POSITION	CENTRAL
HEIGHT	1.88 M
WEIGHT	70 KG
PREFERRED FOOT	RIGHT

APPEARANCES
235

BLOCKS
149

INTERCEPTIONS
251

AERIAL DUELS WON
68.6%

PASS COMPLETION
92%

PENALTIES SCORED
0

GOALS
10

KEY PASSES
37

CLEARANCES
777

TACKLES
226

MAJOR CLUB HONOURS
⚽ Premier League: 2018, 2019, 2021
⚽ UEFA Champions League: runner-up 2021
⚽ FA Cup: 2019

INTERNATIONAL HONOURS
⚽ UEFA European Championship: runner-up 2020
⚽ UEFA Nations League: third place 2019

ACTIVITY AREAS

2

NATIONALITY
French

CURRENT CLUB
Bayern Munich

DAYOT UPAMECANO

Dayot Upamecano has developed into an exceptional centre-half with all the talents needed for the position. His standout talent is his ability with the ball at his feet — a quality that complements his passing accuracy.

BIRTHDATE	27/10/1998
POSITION	CENTRAL
HEIGHT	1.86 M
WEIGHT	90 KG
PREFERRED FOOT	RIGHT

BLOCKS
71

APPEARANCES
177

INTERCEPTIONS
293

AERIAL DUELS WON
62.2%

PASS COMPLETION
87%

PENALTIES SCORED
0

GOALS
5

KEY PASSES
47

CLEARANCES
577

TACKLES
355

MAJOR CLUB HONOURS
⚽ DFL Supercup: 2021

INTERNATIONAL HONOURS
⚽ UEFA Nations League: 2021
⚽ UEFA European U-17 Championship: 2015

ACTIVITY AREAS

RAPHAËL VARANE

While most defenders shine in their late 20s, Raphaël Varane was already a star in his teens. Accurate with either foot, an excellent tackler and great in the air, Varane can also launch attacks with his sharp passing and even score goals.

NATIONALITY
French

CURRENT CLUB
Manchester United

19

BIRTHDATE	25/04/1993
POSITION	CENTRAL
HEIGHT	1.91 M
WEIGHT	81 KG
PREFERRED FOOT	RIGHT

APPEARANCES
365

BLOCKS
182

INTERCEPTIONS
523

AERIAL DUELS WON
69.8%

PENALTIES SCORED
0

PASS COMPLETION
88.1%

GOALS
12

KEY PASSES
60

TACKLES
432

CLEARANCES
1589

MAJOR CLUB HONOURS
⚽ La Liga: 2012, 2017, 2020 (R. Madrid)
⚽ UEFA Champions League: 2014, 2016, 2017, 2018 (R. Madrid)
⚽ UEFA Super Cup: 2014, 2016, 2017 (R. Madrid)
⚽ FIFA Club World Cup: 2014, 2016, 2017, 2018 (R. Madrid)

INTERNATIONAL HONOURS
⚽ FIFA World Cup: 2018
⚽ UEFA Nations League: 2021

ACTIVITY AREAS

MIDFIELDERS

Midfielders are the heartbeat of a team. Not only do they play between the forwards and the defenders but they also help out their team-mates at both ends. Midfielders fall into one of four main categories: 1) defensive midfielders, who sit in front of the back four and are great tacklers; 2) the attacking full-backs operating on the wings, who whip crosses into the box; 3) the central midfielders, who are brilliant at setting up and then joining attacks, as well as helping out in defence whenever needed; 4) the playmakers — these are the stars who build the attack with their creative play.

WHAT DO THE STATS MEAN?

ASSISTS
A pass, cross or header to a team-mate who then scores counts as an assist. This stat also includes a deflected shot that is converted by a team-mate.

SHOTS
Any deliberate strike on goal counts as a shot. The strike does not have to be on target or force a save from the keeper.

CHANCES CREATED
Any pass that results in a shot at goal (whether or not the goal is scored) is regarded as a chance created.

TACKLES
This is the number of times the player has challenged and dispossessed the opposition without committing a foul.

DRIBBLES
This is the number of times the player has gone past an opponent while running with the ball.

75%
SUCCESSFUL PASSES
This shows as a percentage how successful the midfielder is at finding team-mates with passes, whether over five or 60 yards.

Did you know?

In top-level football, midfielders tend to cover the most ground during the course of a match. A midfielder playing the full 90 minutes will usually run anywhere between 9.5 and 12km.

17

NATIONALITY
Belgian

CURRENT CLUB
Manchester City

KEVIN DE BRUYNE

Kevin De Bruyne ranks as one of the finest attacking midfielders in the game today. Strong and technically brilliant, he can break up play at one end and almost immediately blast a 25-metre shot into the opposite goal.

BIRTHDATE	28/06/1991
POSITION	ATTACKING
HEIGHT	1.81 M
WEIGHT	68 KG
PREFERRED FOOT	RIGHT

ASSISTS
138

APPEARANCES
357

DRIBBLES
1118

PASSES
17571
SUCCESSFUL PASSES
80.4%

PENALTIES SCORED
5

GOALS
92

SHOTS
872

CHANCES CREATED
1030

TACKLES
447

MAJOR CLUB HONOURS
⚽ Premier League: 2018, 2019, 2021
⚽ UEFA Champions League: runner-up 2021
⚽ FA Cup: 2019

INTERNATIONAL HONOURS
⚽ FIFA World Cup: third place 2018

ACTIVITY AREAS

SERGIO BUSQUETS

Sergio Busquets plays as a deep midfielder who dictates the team's build-up play with clever, short and longer passes. He is great at stopping attacks before they become dangerous and then making passes to launch his team's raids.

NATIONALITY
Spanish

CURRENT CLUB
Barcelona

5

BIRTHDATE	16/07/1988
POSITION	DEFENSIVE
HEIGHT	1.89 M
WEIGHT	76 KG
PREFERRED FOOT	RIGHT

ASSISTS
36

APPEARANCES
574

DRIBBLES
405

PENALTIES SCORED
0

PASSES
41305
SUCCESSFUL PASSES
90.8%

GOALS
14

SHOTS
138

CHANCES CREATED
356

TACKLES
1480

MAJOR CLUB HONOURS
⚽ La Liga: 2009, 2010, 2011, 2013, 2015, 2016, 2018, 2019 ⚽ UEFA Champions League: 2009, 2011, 2015
⚽ UEFA Super Cup: 2009, 2011, 2015 ⚽ FIFA Club World Cup: 2009, 2011, 2015

INTERNATIONAL HONOURS
⚽ FIFA World Cup: 2010 ⚽ UEFA European Championship: 2012 ⚽ FIFA Confederations Cup: runner up 2013 ⚽ UEFA Nations League: runner-up 2021

ACTIVITY AREAS

23

NATIONALITY
German

CURRENT CLUB
Borussia Dortmund

EMRE CAN

Having been a defender earlier in his career, Emre Can has grown into a classy central midfielder. He combines his excellent tackling strength with his midfielder's instincts to thread passes to team-mates in attacking positions.

BIRTHDATE	12/01/1994
POSITION	CENTRAL
HEIGHT	1.86 M
WEIGHT	86 KG
PREFERRED FOOT	RIGHT

ASSISTS
17

APPEARANCES
295

DRIBBLES
550

PASSES
14558
SUCCESSFUL PASSES
84.1%

PENALTIES SCORED
4

GOALS
26

SHOTS
281

CHANCES CREATED
191

TACKLES
642

MAJOR CLUB HONOURS

⚽ Bundesliga: 2013 (Bayern Munich) ⚽ UEFA Champions League: 2013 (Bayern Munich), runner-up 2018 (Liverpool) ⚽ UEFA Europa League: runner-up 2016 (Liverpool) ⚽ Serie A: 2019, 2020 (Juventus)

INTERNATIONAL HONOURS

⚽ FIFA Confederations Cup: 2017

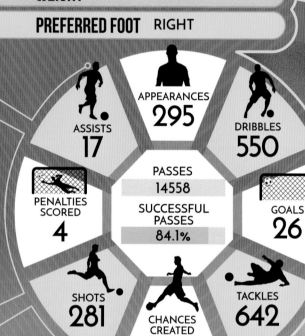

ACTIVITY AREAS

CASEMIRO

Casemiro's strengths are great energy, a high work rate and good support play. Strong, mobile and hard-tackling, his best position is as a defensive midfielder, though his mobility helps get from box to box and he can also play at centre-back.

NATIONALITY
Brazilian

CURRENT CLUB
Real Madrid

14

BIRTHDATE	23/02/1992
POSITION	CENTRAL
HEIGHT	1.85 M
WEIGHT	84 KG
PREFERRED FOOT	RIGHT

APPEARANCES
295

ASSISTS
22

DRIBBLES
222

PENALTIES SCORED
0

PASSES
15801
SUCCESSFUL PASSES
86.2%

GOALS
31

SHOTS
321

CHANCES CREATED
176

TACKLES
905

MAJOR CLUB HONOURS
⚽ La Liga: 2017, 2020 ⚽ UEFA Champions League: 2014, 2016, 2017, 2018 ⚽ UEFA Super Cup: 2014, 2016, 2017 ⚽ FIFA Club World Cup: 2016, 2017, 2018 ⚽ Copa del Rey: 2014

INTERNATIONAL HONOURS
⚽ FIFA U-20 World Cup: 2011
⚽ Copa América: 2019, runner-up 2021

ACTIVITY AREAS

23

NATIONALITY
Brazilian

CURRENT CLUB
Aston Villa*
*On loan from Barcelona

PHILIPPE COUTINHO

Philippe Coutinho brings Brazilian flair to the pitch whenever he plays. Highly skilled with both feet, he is the type of attacking midfielder opposition defenders hate to face. Coutinho scores an average of almost one goal every four games.

BIRTHDATE	12/06/1992
POSITION	ATTACKING
HEIGHT	1.72 M
WEIGHT	68 KG
PREFERRED FOOT	RIGHT

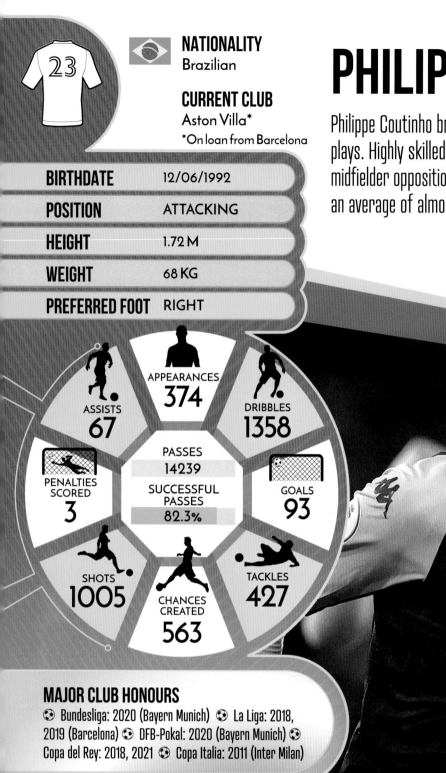

ASSISTS **67**

APPEARANCES **374**

DRIBBLES **1358**

PASSES **14239**
SUCCESSFUL PASSES **82.3%**

PENALTIES SCORED **3**

GOALS **93**

SHOTS **1005**

CHANCES CREATED **563**

TACKLES **427**

MAJOR CLUB HONOURS
⚽ Bundesliga: 2020 (Bayern Munich) ⚽ La Liga: 2018, 2019 (Barcelona) ⚽ DFB-Pokal: 2020 (Bayern Munich) ⚽ Copa del Rey: 2018, 2021 ⚽ Copa Italia: 2011 (Inter Milan)

INTERNATIONAL HONOURS
⚽ Copa América: 2019
⚽ FIFA U-20 World Cup: 2011

ACTIVITY AREAS

JULIAN DRAXLER

Julian Draxler is a thrill to watch! He has the pace to get past the defence and deliver a dangerous cross or pass with pinpoint accuracy. If going for goal himself, he is capable of an impressive left-footed strike.

NATIONALITY
German

CURRENT CLUB
Paris Saint-Germain

BIRTHDATE	20/09/1993
POSITION	ATTACKING
HEIGHT	1.85 M
WEIGHT	72 KG
PREFERRED FOOT	RIGHT

ASSISTS
50

APPEARANCES
358

DRIBBLES
1110

PENALTIES SCORED
0

PASSES
11262
SUCCESSFUL PASSES
86.4%

GOALS
49

SHOTS
449

CHANCES CREATED
440

TACKLES
325

MAJOR CLUB HONOURS
- Ligue 1: 2018, 2019, 2020
- UEFA Champions League: runner-up 2020
- Coupe de France: 2017, 2018, 2020, 2021
- DFB-Pokal: 2011 (Schalke 04)

INTERNATIONAL HONOURS
- FIFA World Cup: 2014
- FIFA Confederations Cup: 2017

ACTIVITY AREAS

3

NATIONALITY
Brazilian

CURRENT CLUB
Liverpool

FABINHO

A hard worker in front of defence, Fabinho is a fan favourite at Liverpool. Tall and strong, he is a master at keeping possession for his team and starting the attack from deep. His heat map shows how dominant he is in midfield.

BIRTHDATE	23/10/1993
POSITION	DEFENSIVE
HEIGHT	1.88 M
WEIGHT	78 KG
PREFERRED FOOT	RIGHT

ASSISTS
19

APPEARANCES
343

DRIBBLES
406

PENALTIES SCORED
19

PASSES
17519

SUCCESSFUL PASSES
85%

GOALS
33

SHOTS
196

CHANCES CREATED
213

TACKLES
899

MAJOR CLUB HONOURS

⚽ Premier League: 2020 ⚽ UEFA Champions League: 2019
⚽ UEFA Super Cup: 2019 ⚽ FIFA Club World Cup: 2019
⚽ Ligue 1: 2017 (Monaco)

INTERNATIONAL HONOURS

⚽ Copa América: 2019, runner-up 2021

ACTIVITY AREAS

BRUNO FERNANDES

Bruno Fernandes shines as a central or attacking midfielder. A sound defensive player, he has a fantastic eye for creating chances with through balls, driving powerful shots from long range and is superb with penalties and free-kicks.

NATIONALITY
Portuguese

CURRENT CLUB
Manchester United

18

BIRTHDATE	08/09/1994
POSITION	ATTACKING
HEIGHT	1.79 M
WEIGHT	69 KG
PREFERRED FOOT	RIGHT

APPEARANCES
251

ASSISTS
58

DRIBBLES
445

PENALTIES SCORED
24

PASSES
10231
SUCCESSFUL PASSES
76.6%

GOALS
74

SHOTS
609

CHANCES CREATED
488

TACKLES
354

MAJOR CLUB HONOURS
- UEFA Europa League: runner-up 2021
- Taça de Portugal: 2019 (Sporting CP)
- Taça de Liga: 2018, 2019 (Sporting CP)

INTERNATIONAL HONOURS
- UEFA Nations League: 2019

ACTIVITY AREAS

NATIONALITY
Brazilian

CURRENT CLUB
Liverpool

ROBERTO FIRMINO

Roberto Firmino is a box-to-box midfielder with great energy and a perfect passing technique over both long and short distances. He usually plays as a second attacker with a superb left foot, but also surprises defenders with his heading ability.

BIRTHDATE	02/10/1991
POSITION	ATT/STRIKER
HEIGHT	1.81 M
WEIGHT	76 KG
PREFERRED FOOT	RIGHT

ASSISTS
82

APPEARANCES
429

DRIBBLES
1613

PENALTIES SCORED
5

PASSES
14619
SUCCESSFUL PASSES
76.9%

GOALS
128

SHOTS
976

CHANCES CREATED
650

TACKLES
776

MAJOR CLUB HONOURS
⚽ Premier League: 2020 ⚽ UEFA Champions League: 2019
⚽ UEFA Europa League: runner-up 2016
⚽ UEFA Super Cup: 2019
⚽ FIFA Club World Cup: 2019

INTERNATIONAL HONOURS
⚽ Copa América: 2019, runner-up 2021

ACTIVITY AREAS

JACK GREALISH

Jack Grealish is among the finest attacking midfielders in Europe. He displays tight ball control, dribbling ability, change of speed and can shoot or deliver dangerous balls into the penalty area from the right or central positions.

NATIONALITY
English

CURRENT CLUB
Manchester City

BIRTHDATE	10/05/1995
POSITION	ATT/STRIKER
HEIGHT	1.75 M
WEIGHT	68 KG
PREFERRED FOOT	RIGHT

APPEARANCES
123

ASSISTS
20

DRIBBLES
401

PENALTIES SCORED
0

PASSES
4017

SUCCESSFUL PASSES
86%

GOALS
18

SHOTS
195

CHANCES CREATED
258

TACKLES
97

MAJOR CLUB HONOURS
⚽ FA Cup: runner-up 2015 (Aston Villa)

INTERNATIONAL HONOURS
⚽ UEFA European Championship: runner-up 2020

ACTIVITY AREAS

7

NATIONALITY
Belgian

CURRENT CLUB
Real Madrid

EDEN HAZARD

Playing as an attacking midfielder or winger, Eden Hazard is one of the best at running with the ball and taking players on. Although hampered by injury the past couple of seasons, his technical brilliance makes him a game changer.

BIRTHDATE	07/01/1991
POSITION	SECOND STRIKER
HEIGHT	1.75 M
WEIGHT	74 KG
PREFERRED FOOT	BOTH

ASSISTS
110

APPEARANCES
528

DRIBBLES
2730

PASSES
21256

SUCCESSFUL PASSES
83.7%

PENALTIES SCORED
32

GOALS
139

SHOTS
912

CHANCES CREATED
1091

TACKLES
318

MAJOR CLUB HONOURS
- ⚽ La Liga: 2020 ⚽ Premier League: 2015, 2017 (Chelsea)
- ⚽ Ligue 1: 2011 (Lille)
- ⚽ UEFA Europa League: 2013, 2019 (Chelsea)
- ⚽ FIFA Club World Cup: runner-up 2012 (Chelsea)

INTERNATIONAL HONOURS
- ⚽ FIFA World Cup: third place 2018

HEAT ROY

ACTIVITY AREAS

FRENKIE DE JONG

Frenkie de Jong has been an outstanding talent ever since he burst on to the scene as a teenager. His close control, accuracy, work rate, passing accuracy and movement have seen him being compared to the great Johan Cruyff.

NATIONALITY
Dutch

CURRENT CLUB
Barcelona

21

BIRTHDATE	12/05/1997
POSITION	CENTRAL
HEIGHT	1.80 M
WEIGHT	74 KG
PREFERRED FOOT	RIGHT

APPEARANCES
133

ASSISTS
12

DRIBBLES
250

PENALTIES SCORED
0

PASSES
8179

SUCCESSFUL PASSES
91.6%

GOALS
9

SHOTS
50

CHANCES CREATED
138

TACKLES
164

MAJOR CLUB HONOURS
- ⚽ UEFA Europa League: runner-up 2017 (Ajax)
- ⚽ Copa del Rey: 2021
- ⚽ Eredivisie: 2019 (Ajax)
- ⚽ KNVB Cup: 2019 (Ajax)

INTERNATIONAL HONOURS
- ⚽ UEFA Nations League: runner-up: 2019

ACTIVITY AREAS

5

NATIONALITY
Italian

CURRENT CLUB
Chelsea

JORGINHO

With Jorginho's midfield talents on show, it was no surprise that both his club and country won their premier continental crowns in summer 2021. He is blessed with a fine positional sense, great tackling technique and passing ability too.

BIRTHDATE	20/12/1991
POSITION	DEFENSIVE MID
HEIGHT	1.80 M
WEIGHT	65 KG
PREFERRED FOOT	RIGHT

ASSISTS
25

APPEARANCES
323

DRIBBLES
258

PENALTIES SCORED
29

PASSES
24685
SUCCESSFUL PASSES
89.4%

GOALS
34

SHOTS
149

CHANCES CREATED
351

TACKLES
666

MAJOR CLUB HONOURS
- ⚽ UEFA Champions League: 2021
- ⚽ UEFA Europa League: 2019
- ⚽ FIFA World Club Cup: 2021
- ⚽ UEFA Super Cup: 2021

INTERNATIONAL HONOURS
- ⚽ UEFA European Championship: 2020

ACTIVITY AREAS

N'GOLO KANTÉ

Defensive midfielder N'Golo Kanté has pace, boundless energy and great positional awareness. He frequently breaks up attacks with timely tackles, blocks and interceptions, then makes accurate passes. He has a decent eye for goal too.

NATIONALITY
French

CURRENT CLUB
Chelsea

7

BIRTHDATE	29/03/1991
POSITION	CENTRAL
HEIGHT	1.68 M
WEIGHT	68 KG
PREFERRED FOOT	RIGHT

APPEARANCES
290

ASSISTS
23

DRIBBLES
579

PENALTIES SCORED
0

PASSES
14349
SUCCESSFUL PASSES
86%

GOALS
14

SHOTS
192

CHANCES CREATED
279

TACKLES
897

MAJOR CLUB HONOURS
⚽ Premier League: 2016 (Leicester City), 2017 ⚽ UEFA Champions League: 2021 ⚽ UEFA Europa League: 2019 ⚽ FIFA Club World Cup: 2021 ⚽ UEFA Super Cup: 2021 ⚽ FA Cup: 2018

INTERNATIONAL HONOURS
⚽ FIFA World Cup: 2018
⚽ UEFA European Championship: runner-up 2016

ACTIVITY AREAS

47

8

TONI KROOS

A set piece specialist who wins challenges in both boxes and dictates the game, Toni Kroos is an athletic box-to-box midfielder who can can pass long and short with either foot. He possesses great vision, creativity and energy.

BIRTHDATE	04/01/1990
POSITION	CENTRAL
HEIGHT	1.83 M
WEIGHT	78 KG
PREFERRED FOOT	RIGHT

APPEARANCES
538

ASSISTS
113

DRIBBLES
610

PASSES
33775

SUCCESSFUL PASSES
91.9%

PENALTIES SCORED
0

GOALS
54

SHOTS
804

CHANCES CREATED
1113

TACKLES
988

MAJOR CLUB HONOURS

⚽ La Liga: 2017, 2020 ⚽ Bundesliga: 2008, 2013, 2014 (B. Mun.) ⚽ UEFA Champions League: 2013 (B. Mun.), 2016, 2017, 2018 ⚽ FIFA Club WC: 2013 (B. Mun.), 2014, 2016, 2017, 2018 ⚽ UEFA Super Cup: 2013 (B. Mun), 2014, 2017

INTERNATIONAL HONOURS

⚽ FIFA World Cup: 2014

ACTIVITY AREAS

SERGEJ MILINKOVIĆ-SAVIĆ

Effective in and around both penalty areas, Sergej Milinković-Savić is a top-class midfielder. He is blessed with great energy and sound technique, and is also good at stopping opposition attacks and launching his own team's raids.

NATIONALITY
Serbian

CURRENT CLUB
Lazio

21

BIRTHDATE	27/02/1995
POSITION	CENTRAL
HEIGHT	1.91 M
WEIGHT	76 KG
PREFERRED FOOT	RIGHT

APPEARANCES
264

ASSISTS
40

DRIBBLES
548

PENALTIES SCORED
0

PASSES
12287

SUCCESSFUL PASSES
77.6%

GOALS
51

SHOTS
539

CHANCES CREATED
339

TACKLES
431

MAJOR CLUB HONOURS
⚽ Coppa Italia: 2019

INTERNATIONAL HONOURS
⚽ UEFA European U-19 Championship: 2013
⚽ FIFA U-20 World Cup: 2015

ACTIVITY AREAS

10

NATIONALITY
Croatian

CURRENT CLUB
Real Madrid

LUKA MODRIĆ

Playmaker Luka Modrić is often at the heart of his team's best attacking moves. He has a great footballing brain, can deliver long and short passes with both feet and strike powerful long-range shots, especially free-kicks.

BIRTHDATE	09/09/1985
POSITION	ATTACKING
HEIGHT	1.72 M
WEIGHT	66 KG
PREFERRED FOOT	RIGHT

ASSISTS
76

APPEARANCES
533

DRIBBLES
1351

PASSES
30055

SUCCESSFUL PASSES
88.6%

PENALTIES SCORED
4

GOALS
45

SHOTS
662

CHANCES CREATED
833

TACKLES
737

MAJOR CLUB HONOURS
- La Liga: 2017, 2020
- UEFA Champions League: 2014, 2016, 2017, 2018
- UEFA Super Cup: 2014, 2016, 2017
- FIFA Club World Cup: 2014, 2016, 2017, 2018

INTERNATIONAL HONOURS
- FIFA World Cup: runner-up 2018

ACTIVITY AREAS

THOMAS MÜLLER

Thomas Müller is a dangerous attacking midfielder, who scores countless goals playing just behind a lone striker. The German powerhouse is mentally strong, tactically clever and great at finding holes in the opposition's defence.

NATIONALITY
German

CURRENT CLUB
Bayern Munich

25

BIRTHDATE	13/09/1989
POSITION	SECOND STRIKER
HEIGHT	1.86 M
WEIGHT	75 KG
PREFERRED FOOT	RIGHT

APPEARANCES
544

ASSISTS
172

DRIBBLES
1001

PASSES
17998
SUCCESSFUL
PASSES
76.7%

PENALTIES
SCORED
22

GOALS
188

SHOTS
1087

CHANCES
CREATED
1052

TACKLES
588

MAJOR CLUB HONOURS
- Bundesliga: x 10 (between 2010 and 2021)
- UEFA Champions League: 2013, 2020
- UEFA Super Cup: 2013, 2020
- FIFA Club World Cup: 2013, 2020

INTERNATIONAL HONOURS
- FIFA World Cup: 2014, third place 2010

ACTIVITY AREAS

5

NATIONALTIY
French

CURRENT CLUB
Manchester United

PAUL POGBA

Known for his strength, speed and athleticism, Paul Pogba glides across the pitch on and off the ball, stopping attacks at one end before finishing off his team's rapid counter-attack. Good with both feet, Pogba is lethal in front of goal.

BIRTHDATE	15/03/1993
POSITION	CENTRAL
HEIGHT	1.91 M
WEIGHT	84 KG
PREFERRED FOOT	RIGHT

ASSISTS
73

APPEARANCES
369

DRIBBLES
1288

PENALTIES SCORED
10

PASSES
18671

SUCCESSFUL PASSES
83.6%

GOALS
67

SHOTS
829

CHANCES CREATED
498

TACKLES
646

MAJOR CLUB HONOURS
- ⚽ Serie A: 2013, 2014, 2015, 2016 (Juventus)
- ⚽ UEFA Europa League: 2017
- ⚽ Coppa Italia: 2015, 2016 (Juventus)

INTERNATIONAL HONOURS
- ⚽ FIFA World Cup: 2018
- ⚽ UEFA Nations League: 2021

ACTIVITY AREAS

RENATO SANCHES

Renato Sanches can play in almost every midfield position: defensive, wide, central or as a creative playmaker. Calm in possession, he is a fine passer, strong tackler and is not afraid of shooting from distance.

NATIONALITY
Portuguese

CURRENT CLUB
Lille

10

BIRTHDATE	18/08/1997
POSITION	CENTRAL
HEIGHT	1.76 M
WEIGHT	70 KG
PREFERRED FOOT	RIGHT

ASSISTS
10

APPEARANCES
141

DRIBBLES
415

PENALTIES SCORED
0

PASSES
4847
SUCCESSFUL PASSES
85.4%

GOALS
7

SHOTS
131

CHANCES CREATED
116

TACKLES
111

MAJOR CLUB HONOURS
- Ligue 1: 2021
- Bundesliga: 2017, 2019 (Bayern Munich)
- DFB-Pokal: 2019 (Bayern Munich)
- Premeira Liga: 2016 (Benfica)

INTERNATIONAL HONOURS
- UEFA European Championship: 2016

ACTIVITY AREAS

7

NATIONALITY
South Korean

CURRENT CLUB
Tottenham Hotspur

SON HEUNG-MIN

Son Heung-Min is at his best when he plays behind the main striker. Although excellent with both feet, attacking from the right side is his strength and he converts a lot of chances that are set up by knock-downs or passes across the box.

BIRTHDATE	08/07/1992
POSITION	WINGER
HEIGHT	1.83 M
WEIGHT	78 KG
PREFERRED FOOT	BOTH

ASSISTS
63

APPEARANCES
426

DRIBBLES
1299

PENALTIES
SCORED
1

PASSES
10030
SUCCESSFUL
PASSES
81.9%

GOALS
152

SHOTS
920

CHANCES
CREATED
488

TACKLES
348

MAJOR CLUB HONOURS
⚽ UEFA Champions League: runner-up 2019

INTERNATIONAL HONOURS
⚽ AFC Asian Cup: runner-up 2015

ACTIVITY AREAS

MARCO VERRATTI

Marco Verratti is an awesome ball-playing midfielder. He is able to dribble past defenders at speed to set up chances for the players ahead of him. He can pass or shoot accurately and powerfully with both feet.

 **NATIONALITY**
Italian

CURRENT CLUB
Paris Saint-Germain

BIRTHDATE	05/11/1992
POSITION	CENTRAL
HEIGHT	1.65 M
WEIGHT	60 KG
PREFERRED FOOT	RIGHT

APPEARANCES
313

ASSISTS
45

DRIBBLES
626

PENALTIES SCORED
0

PASSES
25610
SUCCESSFUL PASSES
91.2%

GOALS
10

SHOTS
91

CHANCES CREATED
353

TACKLES
861

MAJOR CLUB HONOURS
- Ligue 1: 2013, 2014, 2015, 2016, 2018, 2019, 2020
- UEFA Champions League: runner-up 2020
- Coupe de France: 2015, 2016, 2017, 2018, 2020, 2021

INTERNATIONAL HONOURS
- UEFA European Championship: 2020
- UEFA Nations League: third place 2021

ACTIVITY AREAS

55

18

NATIONALITY
Dutch

CURRENT CLUB
Paris Saint-Germain

GEORGINIO WIJNALDUM

Georginio Wijnaldum can play anywhere in the middle of the pitch as an attacking playmaker or a defensive shield for the back-line. Good with both feet and a strong tackler, he goes box to box and scores crucial goals, especially with headers.

BIRTHDATE	11/11/1990
POSITION	ATTACKING
HEIGHT	1.75 M
WEIGHT	69 KG
PREFERRED FOOT	RIGHT

ASSISTS
21

APPEARANCES
316

DRIBBLES
570

PENALTIES SCORED
2

PASSES
12477
SUCCESSFUL PASSES
89.1%

GOALS
42

SHOTS
353

CHANCES CREATED
237

TACKLES
304

MAJOR CLUB HONOURS
⚽ Premier League: 2020 (Liverpool) ⚽ UEFA Champions League: 2019 (Liverpool), runner-up 2018 (Liverpool) ⚽ UEFA Super Cup: 2019 (Liverpool) ⚽ FIFA Club World Cup: 2019 (Liverpool)

INTERNATIONAL HONOURS
⚽ UEFA Nations League: runner-up 2019
⚽ FIFA World Cup: third place 2014

ACTIVITY AREAS

AXEL WITSEL

Originally a pacy right-winger, Axel Witsel has developed into a strong central midfielder for his club. He frequently drives his team forward with both his play and leadership skills. He is especially good at delivering dangerous passes with either foot.

NATIONALITY
Belgian

CURRENT CLUB
Borussia Dortmund

28

BIRTHDATE	12/01/1989
POSITION	CENTRAL
HEIGHT	1.86 M
WEIGHT	81 KG
PREFERRED FOOT	RIGHT

APPEARANCES
201

ASSISTS
10

DRIBBLES
206

PENALTIES SCORED
1

PASSES
11140
SUCCESSFUL PASSES
91.4%

GOALS
19

SHOTS
188

CHANCES CREATED
102

TACKLES
334

MAJOR CLUB HONOURS
- DFL-Pokal: 2021
- DFL-Supercup: 2019

INTERNATIONAL HONOURS
- FIFA World Cup: third place 2018

ACTIVITY AREAS

FORWARDS

The forwards, or strikers, are a team's frontline attackers and the chief goalscorers. They are also the team's most celebrated players. Whether it is the smaller, quicker player, such as Neymar Jr and Mohamed Salah, or the bigger, more physical attacker, such as Cristiano Ronaldo and Romelu Lukaku, strikers have perfected the ability to find the back of the net on a regular basis. Aside from scoring lots of goals the world's best strikers are also effective in creating chances for their team-mates.

WHAT DO THE STATS MEAN?

GOALS
This is the total number of goals a striker has scored. The figure spans across all the top clubs the player has represented so far in their career.

CONVERSION RATE
The percentage shows how good the player is at taking their chance in front of goal. If a player scores two goals from four shots, their conversion rate is 50%.

ASSISTS
A pass, cross or header to a team-mate who then scores counts as an assist. This stat also includes a deflected shot that is immediately converted by a team-mate.

MINUTES PER GOAL
This is the average length of time it takes for the player to score. It is calculated across all the minutes the player has played in their career at top level.

Did you know?

A perfect hat-trick is one where the player scores one goal with his right foot, another with his left foot and a third with his head. It does not matter in which order the goals come.

NATIONALITY
French

CURRENT CLUB
Real Madrid

KARIM BENZEMA

Karim Benzema is both a creator and scorer of goals. Intelligent with a great work rate, he can play out wide, down the middle or behind the front man. Although right-footed, he scores many goals with his left and his head.

BIRTHDATE	19/12/1987
POSITION	STRIKER
HEIGHT	1.85 M
WEIGHT	81 KG
PREFERRED FOOT	BOTH

GOALS
341

PENALTIES SCORED
22

APPEARANCES
660

ASSISTS
137

CONVERSION RATE
18%

MINUTES PER GOAL
137

GOALS LEFT
62

GOALS RIGHT
219

HAT-TRICKS
8

HEADED GOALS
55

SHOTS
1848

MAJOR CLUB HONOURS
⚽ La Liga: 2012, 2017, 2020 ⚽ FIFA Club World Cup: 2014, 2016, 2017, 2018 ⚽ UEFA Super Cup: 2014, 2016, 2017 ⚽ UEFA Champions League: 2014, 2016, 2017, 2018 ⚽ Ligue 1: 2005, 2006, 2007, 2008 (Lyon)

INTERNATIONAL HONOURS
⚽ UEFA Nations League: 2021

ACTIVITY AREAS

EDINSON CAVANI

Edinson Cavani is a fine dribbler, great at running into space and scoring spectacular goals, especially with overhead kicks. He has an impressive work rate, too, always hassling the opposition's defence to win the ball.

NATIONALITY
Uruguayan

CURRENT CLUB
Manchester United

BIRTHDATE	14/02/1987
POSITION	STRIKER
HEIGHT	1.84 M
WEIGHT	71 KG
PREFERRED FOOT	RIGHT

GOALS
315

PENALTIES SCORED
45

ASSISTS
56

APPEARANCES
543

CONVERSION RATE
20%

MINUTES PER GOAL
129

GOALS LEFT
49

GOALS RIGHT
209

HAT-TRICKS
14

HEADED GOALS
54

SHOTS
1,589

MAJOR CLUB HONOURS
- ⚽ UEFA Champions League: runner-up 2020 (PSG)
- ⚽ UEFA Europa League: runner-up 2021
- ⚽ Ligue 1: 2014, 2015, 2016, 2018, 2019, 2020 (PSG)
- ⚽ Coupe de France: 2015, 2016, 2017, 2018, 2020 (PSG)

INTERNATIONAL HONOURS
- ⚽ Copa América: 2011

ACTIVITY AREAS

9

NATIONALITY
Dutch

CURRENT CLUB
Barcelona

MEMPHIS DEPAY

Memphis Depay has developed into a world-class striker, though he is still considered to be a left-winger or left-sided striker. He is a brave player and will challenge the biggest defenders in the middle of the danger area.

BIRTHDATE	13/02/1994
POSITION	WINGER
HEIGHT	1.76 M
WEIGHT	78 KG
PREFERRED FOOT	RIGHT

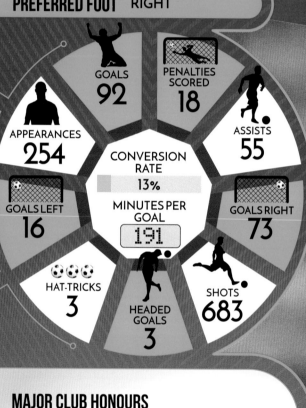

GOALS
92

PENALTIES SCORED
18

APPEARANCES
254

ASSISTS
55

CONVERSION RATE
13%

MINUTES PER GOAL
191

GOALS LEFT
16

GOALS RIGHT
73

HAT-TRICKS
3

HEADED GOALS
3

SHOTS
683

MAJOR CLUB HONOURS
⚽ Eredivisie: 2015 (PSV Eindhoven)
⚽ KNVB Cup: 2012 (PSV Eindhoven)

INTERNATIONAL HONOURS
⚽ FIFA World Cup: third place 2014

ACTIVITY AREAS

JOÃO FÉLIX

The latest great young striker to emerge out of Portugal, João Félix has developed into a regular goalscorer in La Liga. His tactical intelligence, energy and versatility mean he can be very effective as a central striker, second forward, attacking midfielder or winger.

NATIONALITY
Portuguese

CURRENT CLUB
Atlético Madrid

BIRTHDATE	10/11/1999
POSITION	FORWARD
HEIGHT	1.81 M
WEIGHT	70 KG
PREFERRED FOOT	RIGHT

GOALS
31

PENALTIES SCORED
4

ASSISTS
13

APPEARANCES
109

CONVERSION RATE
15%

MINUTES PER GOAL
217

GOALS RIGHT
23

GOALS LEFT
5

HAT-TRICKS
1

HEADED GOALS
3

SHOTS
210

MAJOR CLUB HONOURS
- La Liga: 2021
- Primeira Liga: 2019 (Benfica)

INTERNATIONAL HONOURS
- UEFA Nations League: 2019

ACTIVITY AREAS

63

9

NATIONALITY
Norwegian

CURRENT CLUB
Borussia Dortmund

ERLING HAALAND

Erling Haaland has become one of the most exciting and promising forwards in world football. He has all the talents: two good feet, blistering pace, good in the air, energy, strength, timing and the instincts to get into scoring positions.

BIRTHDATE	21/07/2000
POSITION	STRIKER
HEIGHT	1.94 M
WEIGHT	88 KG
PREFERRED FOOT	LEFT

GOALS
79

PENALTIES SCORED
8

ASSISTS
17

APPEARANCES
82

CONVERSION RATE
32%

MINUTES PER GOAL
81

GOALS LEFT
60

GOALS RIGHT
11

HAT-TRICKS
3

HEADED GOALS
8

SHOTS
249

MAJOR CLUB HONOURS
- DFB-Pokal: 2021
- Austrian Bundesliga: 2019, 2020 (Red Bull Salzburg)
- Austrian Cup: 2019 (Red Bull Salzburg)

INTERNATIONAL HONOURS
- None to date

ACTIVITY AREAS

ZLATAN IBRAHIMOVIĆ

NATIONALITY
Swedish

CURRENT CLUB
AC Milan

Zlatan Ibrahimović is one of world football's most recognisable strikers. He is supremely self-confident, amazingly agile — overhead scissors kicks are a trademark — and he scores with either foot or head, from close in, long range, set pieces and open play.

BIRTHDATE	03/10/1981
POSITION	STRIKER
HEIGHT	1.95 M
WEIGHT	95 KG
PREFERRED FOOT	RIGHT

GOALS
354

PENALTIES SCORED
63

ASSISTS
137

APPEARANCES
599

CONVERSION RATE
16%

MINUTES PER GOAL
134

GOALS LEFT
58

GOALS RIGHT
252

HAT-TRICKS
11

HEADED GOALS
37

SHOTS
2252

MAJOR CLUB HONOURS
⚽ Serie A: 2007, 2008, 2009 (Inter Milan), 2011 (Milan) ⚽
La Liga: 2010 (Barca) ⚽ FIFA Club World Cup: 2009 (Barca) ⚽
UEFA Super Cup: 2009 (Barca) ⚽ UEFA Europa League: 2017 (Man.
Utd) ⚽ Ligue 1: 2013, 2014, 2015, 2016 (PSG)

INTERNATIONAL HONOURS
⚽ None to date

ACTIVITY AREAS

17

NATIONALITY
Italian

CURRENT CLUB
Lazio

CIRO IMMOBILE

A great team-player, Ciro Immobile is a natural finisher who is excellent in the air. His goals tally is even higher because he refuses to give up lost causes and is willing to chase back to force mistakes out of defenders.

BIRTHDATE	20/02/1990
POSITION	STRIKER
HEIGHT	1.85 M
WEIGHT	78 KG
PREFERRED FOOT	RIGHT

GOALS
208

PENALTIES SCORED
49

ASSISTS
49

APPEARANCES
359

CONVERSION RATE
19%

MINUTES PER GOAL
128

GOALS LEFT
26

GOALS RIGHT
160

HAT-TRICKS
8

HEADED GOALS
22

SHOTS
1084

MAJOR CLUB HONOURS
⚽ Coppa Italia: 2019

INTERNATIONAL HONOURS
🌐 UEFA European Championship: 2020

ACTIVITY AREAS

DIOGO JOTA

Most effective as a main striker, Diogo Jota is able to adapt his game to play deeper or as a left-winger. He'll wait for defenders to be dragged out of position before running into spaces behind them and shooting powerfully with his right foot.

NATIONALITY
Portuguese

CURRENT CLUB
Liverpool

20

BIRTHDATE	04/12/1996
POSITION	STRIKER
HEIGHT	1.78 M
WEIGHT	68 KG
PREFERRED FOOT	BOTH

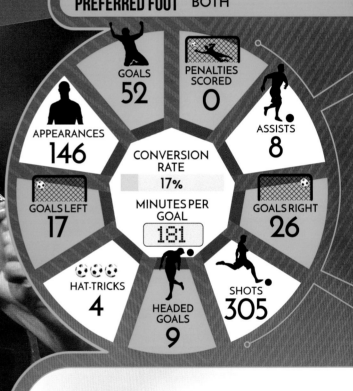

GOALS
52

PENALTIES SCORED
0

ASSISTS
8

APPEARANCES
146

CONVERSION RATE
17%

MINUTES PER GOAL
181

GOALS LEFT
17

GOALS RIGHT
26

HAT-TRICKS
4

HEADED GOALS
9

SHOTS
305

MAJOR CLUB HONOURS
⚽ English Football League Cup: 2022

INTERNATIONAL HONOURS
⚽ UEFA Nations League: 2019

ACTIVITY AREAS

67

16

NATIONALITY
Serbian

CURRENT CLUB
Real Madrid

LUKA JOVIĆ

Luka Jović is a predator in the penalty box. He uses his speed and attacking instincts to find spaces in the penalty area and score goals from close range with deft touches from either foot and, occasionally, his head.

BIRTHDATE	23/12/1997
POSITION	STRIKER
HEIGHT	1.73 M
WEIGHT	70 KG
PREFERRED FOOT	RIGHT

GOALS
42

PENALTIES SCORED
1

ASSISTS
10

APPEARANCES
130

CONVERSION RATE
17%

MINUTES PER GOAL
147

GOALS LEFT
14

GOALS RIGHT
20

HAT-TRICKS
1

HEADED GOALS
8

SHOTS
248

MAJOR CLUB HONOURS
⚽ La Liga: 2020
⚽ DFB-Pokal: 2018 (Eintracht Frankfurt)

INTERNATIONAL HONOURS
⚽ None to date

ACTIVITY AREAS

HARRY KANE

Harry Kane has developed his game to become a complete striker. His power in the air, physical strength and technical ability with both feet make him hard to stop, and he also sets up many goals for his team-mates.

NATIONALITY
English

CURRENT CLUB
Tottenham Hotspur

10

BIRTHDATE	28/07/1993
POSITION	STRIKER
HEIGHT	1.88 M
WEIGHT	86 KG
PREFERRED FOOT	RIGHT

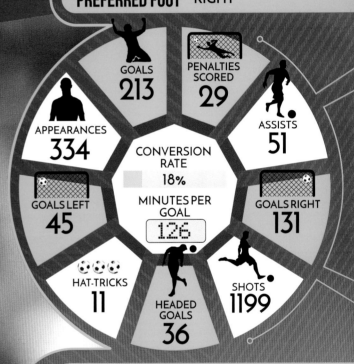

GOALS
213

PENALTIES SCORED
29

ASSISTS
51

APPEARANCES
334

CONVERSION RATE
18%

MINUTES PER GOAL
126

GOALS LEFT
45

GOALS RIGHT
131

HAT-TRICKS
11

HEADED GOALS
36

SHOTS
1199

MAJOR CLUB HONOURS
⚽ UEFA Champions League: runner-up 2019

INTERNATIONAL HONOURS
⚽ UEFA European Championship: runner-up 2020
⚽ UEFA Nations League: third place 2019

ACTIVITY AREAS

9

NATIONALITY
Polish

CURRENT CLUB
Bayern Munich

ROBERT LEWANDOWSKI

Robert Lewandowski has consistently ranked as one of the world's best strikers since he made his debut at Borussia Dortmund in 2010. His positioning, technique, power and finishing have seen him net more than 300 goals in the Bundesliga.

BIRTHDATE	21/08/1988
POSITION	STRIKER
HEIGHT	1.84 M
WEIGHT	80 KG
PREFERRED FOOT	RIGHT

GOALS
396

PENALTIES SCORED
56

APPEARANCES
498

ASSISTS
73

CONVERSION RATE
21%

MINUTES PER GOAL
102

GOALS LEFT
64

GOALS RIGHT
264

HAT-TRICKS
21

HEADED GOALS
64

SHOTS
1918

MAJOR CLUB HONOURS
⚽ Bundesliga: 2011, 2012 (B. Dortmund), 2015, 2016, 2017, 2018, 2019, 2020, 2021 ⚽ UEFA Champions League: 2020
⚽ DFB-Pokal: 2012 (B. Dortmund), 2016, 2019, 2020 ⚽ FIFA Club World Cup: 2020 ⚽ UEFA Super Cup: 2020

INTERNATIONAL HONOURS
⚽ None to date

ACTIVITY AREAS

ROMELU LUKAKU

Romelu Lukaku often uses his size and strength to dispossess defenders before controlling the ball and unleashing a fierce shot or a pass to a well-placed team-mate. He is also superb in the air and scores many headers.

NATIONALITY
Belgian

CURRENT CLUB
Chelsea

BIRTHDATE	13/05/1993
POSITION	STRIKER
HEIGHT	1.90 M
WEIGHT	94 KG
PREFERRED FOOT	LEFT

GOALS **200**

PENALTIES SCORED **22**

APPEARANCES **410**

ASSISTS **57**

CONVERSION RATE **19%**

MINUTES PER GOAL **155**

GOALS LEFT **110**

GOALS RIGHT **49**

HAT-TRICKS **4**

HEADED GOALS **38**

SHOTS **1063**

MAJOR CLUB HONOURS
- Serie A: 2021 (Inter Milan)
- FIFA Club World Cup 2021
- UEFA Europa League: runner-up 2020 (Inter Milan)
- Belgian Pro League: 2010 (Anderlecht)

INTERNATIONAL HONOURS
- FIFA World Cup: third place 2018

ACTIVITY AREAS

10

NATIONALITY
Senegalese

CURRENT CLUB
Liverpool

SADIO MANÉ

Sadio Mané has breathtaking pace and dribbling ability. Although he normally plays on the wing, he can also be dangerous in the middle of the park as he can leap high to win headers and shoot powerfully with either foot.

BIRTHDATE	10/04/1992
POSITION	WINGER
HEIGHT	1.75 M
WEIGHT	69 KG
PREFERRED FOOT	RIGHT

GOALS
134

PENALTIES SCORED
0

APPEARANCES
317

ASSISTS
44

CONVERSION RATE
18%

MINUTES PER GOAL
186

GOALS LEFT
36

GOALS RIGHT
81

HAT-TRICKS
3

HEADED GOALS
17

SHOTS
735

MAJOR CLUB HONOURS
- ⚽ Premier League: 2020
- ⚽ UEFA Champions League: 2019, runner-up 2018
- ⚽ UEFA Super Cup: 2019
- ⚽ FIFA Club World Cup: 2019

INTERNATIONAL HONOURS
- ⚽ CAF Africa Cup of Nations: 2021, runner-up 2019

ACTIVITY AREAS

KYLIAN MBAPPÉ

A FIFA World Cup winner with France at just 18, Kylian Mbappé is counted among the best strikers in world football today. The pacey finisher is a superb ball-player who consistently gets on the score sheet and sets up chances for his team-mates.

NATIONALITY
French

CURRENT CLUB
Paris Saint-Germain

BIRTHDATE	20/12/1998
POSITION	STRIKER
HEIGHT	1.78 M
WEIGHT	73 KG
PREFERRED FOOT	RIGHT

GOALS
160

PENALTIES SCORED
11

ASSISTS
71

APPEARANCES
230

CONVERSION RATE
22%

MINUTES PER GOAL
105

GOALS LEFT
33

GOALS RIGHT
120

HAT-TRICKS
7

HEADED GOALS
7

SHOTS
730

MAJOR CLUB HONOURS
- ⚽ Ligue 1: 2017 (Monaco), 2018, 2019, 2020
- ⚽ UEFA Champions League: runner-up 2020
- ⚽ Coupe de France: 2018, 2020, 2021

INTERNATIONAL HONOURS
- ⚽ FIFA World Cup: 2018
- ⚽ UEFA Nations League: 2021

ACTIVITY AREAS

30

NATIONALITY
Argentinian

CURRENT CLUB
Paris Saint-Germain

LIONEL MESSI

The greatest player of his generation, if not the greatest ever, Lionel Messi is a fine playmaker with a stunning goal-scoring record. He is also a fantastically fast dribbler who can carve out opportunities to shoot with either foot, from any range.

BIRTHDATE	24/06/1987
POSITION	FORWARD
HEIGHT	1.70 M
WEIGHT	72 KG
PREFERRED FOOT	LEFT

GOALS
602

PENALTIES SCORED
78

APPEARANCES
696

ASSISTS
240

CONVERSION RATE
19%

MINUTES PER GOAL
94

GOALS LEFT
499

GOALS RIGHT
82

HAT-TRICKS
44

HEADED GOALS
20

SHOTS
3122

MAJOR CLUB HONOURS

⚽ La Liga: 2005, 2006, 2009, 2010, 2011, 2013, 2015, 2016, 2018, 2019 (Barca) ⚽ UEFA Champions League: 2006, 2009, 2011, 2015 (Barca) ⚽ UEFA Super Cup: 2009, 2011, 2015 (Barca) ⚽ FIFA Club World Cup: 2009, 2011, 2015 (Barca)

INTERNATIONAL HONOURS

⚽ FIFA World Cup: runner-up 2014
⚽ Olympic Games: gold medal 2008
⚽ Copa América: 2021, runner-up 2007, 2015, 2016

ACTIVITY AREAS

ÁLVARO MORATA

Álvaro Morata is perfectly built for a central striker. Tall, strong and excellent in the air, he is comfortable with the ball at his feet. Morata is also surprisingly fast and has great tactical and positional awareness.

NATIONALITY
Spanish

CURRENT CLUB
Juventus

BIRTHDATE	23/10/1992
POSITION	STRIKER
HEIGHT	1.90 M
WEIGHT	84 KG
PREFERRED FOOT	RIGHT

GOALS 118

PENALTIES SCORED 5

APPEARANCES 355

ASSISTS 47

CONVERSION RATE 17%

MINUTES PER GOAL 163

GOALS LEFT 26

GOALS RIGHT 60

HAT-TRICKS 2

HEADED GOALS 32

SHOTS 682

MAJOR CLUB HONOURS
⚽ La Liga: 2012, 2017 (R. Mad..) ⚽ Serie A: 2015, 2016 ⚽ UEFA Champions League: 2014, 2017 (R. Mad.), runner-up 2015 ⚽ UEFA Europa League: 2019 (Chelsea) ⚽ UEFA Super Cup: 2016 (R. Mad..) ⚽ FIFA Club World Cup: 2016 (R. Mad.)

INTERNATIONAL HONOURS
⚽ UEFA European U-21 Championship: 2013

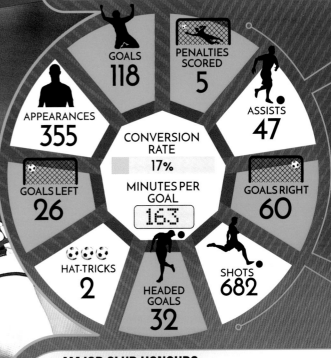

ACTIVITY AREAS

10

NATIONALITY
Brazilian

CURRENT CLUB
Paris Saint-Germain

NEYMAR JR

Neymar is the latest in the long line of great Brazilian strikers. His pace and phenomenal dribbling help him beat defenders in numbers. He strikes fear into the opposition defence with his energetic pace and playmaking skills.

BIRTHDATE	05/02/1992
POSITION	FORWARD
HEIGHT	1.75 M
WEIGHT	68 KG
PREFERRED FOOT	RIGHT

GOALS
175

PENALTIES SCORED
31

ASSISTS
101

APPEARANCES
285

CONVERSION RATE
18%

MINUTES PER GOAL
136

GOALS LEFT
47

GOALS RIGHT
122

HAT-TRICKS
8

HEADED GOALS
6

SHOTS
959

MAJOR CLUB HONOURS
⚽ La Liga: 2015, 2016, 2017 (Barca) ⚽ Ligue 1: 2018, 2019, 2020 ⚽ UEFA Champions League: 2016 (Barca) ⚽ FIFA Club World Cup: 2016 (Barca) ⚽ Copa del Rey: 2015, 2016, 2017 (Barca) ⚽ Coupe de France: 2018, 2020, 2021

INTERNATIONAL HONOURS
⚽ Copa América: runner-up 2021
⚽ FIFA Confederations Cup: 2013
⚽ Olympic Games: silver medal 2012, gold medal 2016

ACTIVITY AREAS

MARCO REUS

Marco Reus is an attacker who can lead the front line, play as a second striker or out wide. He is an expert finisher, especially with his right foot, and is also fantastic at setting up chances for his team-mates.

NATIONALITY
German

CURRENT CLUB
Borussia Dortmund

BIRTHDATE	31/05/1989
POSITION	FORWARD
HEIGHT	1.80 M
WEIGHT	71 KG
PREFERRED FOOT	RIGHT

GOALS
170

PENALTIES SCORED
16

ASSISTS
94

APPEARANCES
407

CONVERSION RATE
17%

GOALS RIGHT
124

GOALS LEFT
40

MINUTES PER GOAL
189

HAT-TRICKS
3

HEADED GOALS
6

SHOTS
1011

MAJOR CLUB HONOURS
⚽ UEFA Champions League: runner-up 2013
⚽ DFB-Pokal: 2017, 2021

INTERNATIONAL HONOURS
⚽ None to date

ACTIVITY AREAS

7

NATIONALITY
Portuguese

CURRENT CLUB
Manchester United

CRISTIANO RONALDO

The superstar striker has wowed fans across the world with his all-round attacking skills. He is breathtaking to watch when he is running at defences, brilliant in the air and a superb finisher, with an extraordinary goal-scoring record.

BIRTHDATE	05/02/1985
POSITION	FORWARD
HEIGHT	1.87 M
WEIGHT	83 KG
PREFERRED FOOT	RIGHT

GOALS
628

PENALTIES SCORED
116

APPEARANCES
796

ASSISTS
180

CONVERSION RATE
14%

MINUTES PER GOAL
105

GOALS LEFT
106

GOALS RIGHT
418

HAT-TRICKS
46

HEADED GOALS
102

SHOTS
4467

MAJOR CLUB HONOURS

⚽ EPL: 2007–09 ⚽ UEFA Champs League: 2008 (Man. U), 2014, 2016–18 (R. Mad.) ⚽ FIFA Club World Cup: 2008 (Man. U), 2014, 2016–17 (R. Mad.) ⚽ UEFA Super Cup: 2014, 2017 (R. Mad.) ⚽ Serie A: 2019, 2020 (Juve) ⚽ La Liga: 2012, 2017 (R. Mad.)

INTERNATIONAL HONOURS

⚽ UEFA European Championship: 2016
⚽ UEFA Nations League: 2019

ACTIVITY AREAS

MOHAMED SALAH

The two-time African Footballer of the Year is a brilliant left-footed attacker who prowls the left wing. Mo Salah has amazing pace with the ability to make angled runs, finding gaps in defences before scoring spectacular goals.

NATIONALITY
Egyptian

CURRENT CLUB
Liverpool

11

BIRTHDATE	15/06/1992
POSITION	FORWARD
HEIGHT	1.75 M
WEIGHT	71 KG
PREFERRED FOOT	LEFT

GOALS
193

PENALTIES SCORED
22

APPEARANCES
363

ASSISTS
79

CONVERSION RATE
17%

MINUTES PER GOAL
148

GOALS LEFT
156

GOALS RIGHT
30

HAT-TRICKS
5

HEADED GOALS
7

SHOTS
1134

MAJOR CLUB HONOURS
- ⚽ Premier League: 2020
- ⚽ UEFA Champions League: 2019, runner-up 2018
- ⚽ UEFA Super Cup: 2019
- ⚽ FIFA Club World Cup: 2019

INTERNATIONAL HONOURS
- ⚽ CAF Africa Cup of Nations: runner-up (x2) 2017, 2021

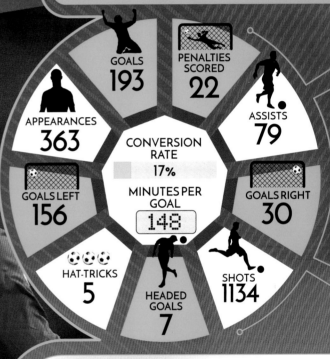

ACTIVITY AREAS

NATIONALITY
English

CURRENT CLUB
Manchester City

RAHEEM STERLING

The England international has matured into the complete forward at Manchester City. No longer a winger, he plays all over the front line but is at his best behind a front man, peeling off the left side and firing shots with his right foot.

BIRTHDATE	08/12/1994
POSITION	FORWARD
HEIGHT	1.70 M
WEIGHT	69 KG
PREFERRED FOOT	RIGHT

GOALS
130

PENALTIES SCORED
3

ASSISTS
70

APPEARANCES
394

CONVERSION RATE
16%

MINUTES PER GOAL
222

GOALS LEFT
35

GOALS RIGHT
85

HAT-TRICKS
6

HEADED GOALS
10

SHOTS
799

MAJOR CLUB HONOURS
⚽ Premier League: 2018, 2019, 2021
⚽ UEFA Champions League: runner-up 2021
⚽ FA Cup: 2019

INTERNATIONAL HONOURS
⚽ UEFA European Championship: runner-up 2020
⚽ UEFA Europa Nations League: third place 2019

ACTIVITY AREAS

LUIS SUÁREZ

Luis Suárez has a talent for scoring spectacular goals with his right foot, either facing or with his back to goal. He loves running at defenders and beating them with pace or dribbling trickery before smashing great shots past goalkeepers.

NATIONALITY
Uruguayan

CURRENT CLUB
Atlético Madrid

BIRTHDATE	24/01/1987
POSITION	FORWARD
HEIGHT	1.82 M
WEIGHT	86 KG
PREFERRED FOOT	RIGHT

GOALS
286

PENALTIES SCORED
19

ASSISTS
122

APPEARANCES
462

CONVERSION RATE
17%

MINUTES PER GOAL
132

GOALS LEFT
57

GOALS RIGHT
196

HAT-TRICKS
16

HEADED GOALS
31

SHOTS
1656

MAJOR CLUB HONOURS
⚽ La Liga: 2015, 2016, 2018, 2019 (Barcelona), 2021 ⚽ UEFA Champions League: 2015 (Barcelona) ⚽ UEFA Super Cup: 2015 (Barcelona) ⚽ FIFA Club World Cup: 2015 (Barcelona) ⚽ Copa del Rey: 2015, 2016, 2017, 2018 (Barcelona)

INTERNATIONAL HONOURS
⚽ Copa América 2011

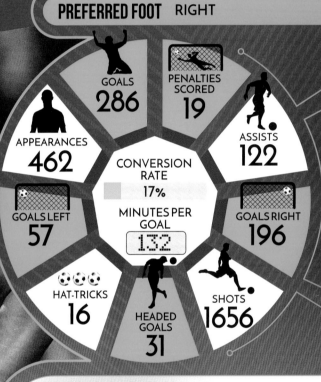

ACTIVITY AREAS

NATIONALITY
English

CURRENT CLUB
Leicester City

JAMIE VARDY

Jamie Vardy came late into top-flight football and is still getting better. Mainly right-footed, he is an old-fashioned goal-scoring No. 9, leading the line with his strength, power and bravery, beating defenders in the air and on the ground.

BIRTHDATE	11/01/1987
POSITION	STRIKER
HEIGHT	1.79 M
WEIGHT	74 KG
PREFERRED FOOT	RIGHT

GOALS
132

PENALTIES SCORED
27

ASSISTS
40

APPEARANCES
280

CONVERSION RATE
22%

MINUTES PER GOAL
171

GOALS RIGHT
85

GOALS LEFT
32

HAT-TRICKS
3

HEADED GOALS
15

SHOTS
601

MAJOR CLUB HONOURS
⚽ Premier League: 2016
⚽ FA Cup: 2021

INTERNATIONAL HONOURS
⚽ None to date

ACTIVITY AREAS

DUŠAN VLAHOVIĆ

One of world football's most exciting rising stars, Dušan Vlahović is very strong and is great in physical battles. He is excellent in the air, winning headers or flicking the ball on, and almost always converts chances close to goal.

NATIONALITY
Serbian

CURRENT CLUB
Juventus

7

BIRTHDATE	28/01/2000
POSITION	STRIKER
HEIGHT	1.90 M
WEIGHT	75 KG
PREFERRED FOOT	LEFT

GOALS
50

PENALTIES SCORED
12

ASSISTS
6

APPEARANCES
109

CONVERSION RATE
18%

MINUTES PER GOAL
147

GOALS LEFT
40

GOALS RIGHT
5

HAT-TRICKS
2

HEADED GOALS
5

SHOTS
273

MAJOR CLUB HONOURS
⚽ Serbian SuperLiga: 2017 (Partizan)

INTERNATIONAL HONOURS
⚽ None to date

ACTIVITY AREAS

83

GOALKEEPERS

The goalkeeper is a team's last line of defence and unlike the other positions there is no one playing next to them. There is more pressure on goalkeepers than in any other position because when a keeper makes an error, the chances are that the other team will score. The goalies featured in this section are all great shot-stoppers, but some play outside their penalty areas as sweeper-keepers; others have made their reputation as penalty-savers; then there are those who are great at catching the ball or punching it clear.

WHAT DO THE STATS MEAN?

CATCHES
This is the number of times the keeper has dealt with an attack – usually a cross – by catching the ball.

CLEAN SHEETS
Any occasion on which the goalie has not let in a goal for the full duration of the game counts as a clean sheet.

GOALS CONCEDED
This is the number of goals the keeper has conceded in their career in top-division football.

PENALTIES FACED/SAVED
This is the number of times a goalie has faced a penalty (excludes shoot-outs) and how successful he has been at saving it.

PUNCHES
This is a measure of how often the keeper has dealt with a dangerous ball (usually a cross) by punching it clear.

SAVES
This shows how many times the goalkeeper has stopped a shot or header that was on target.

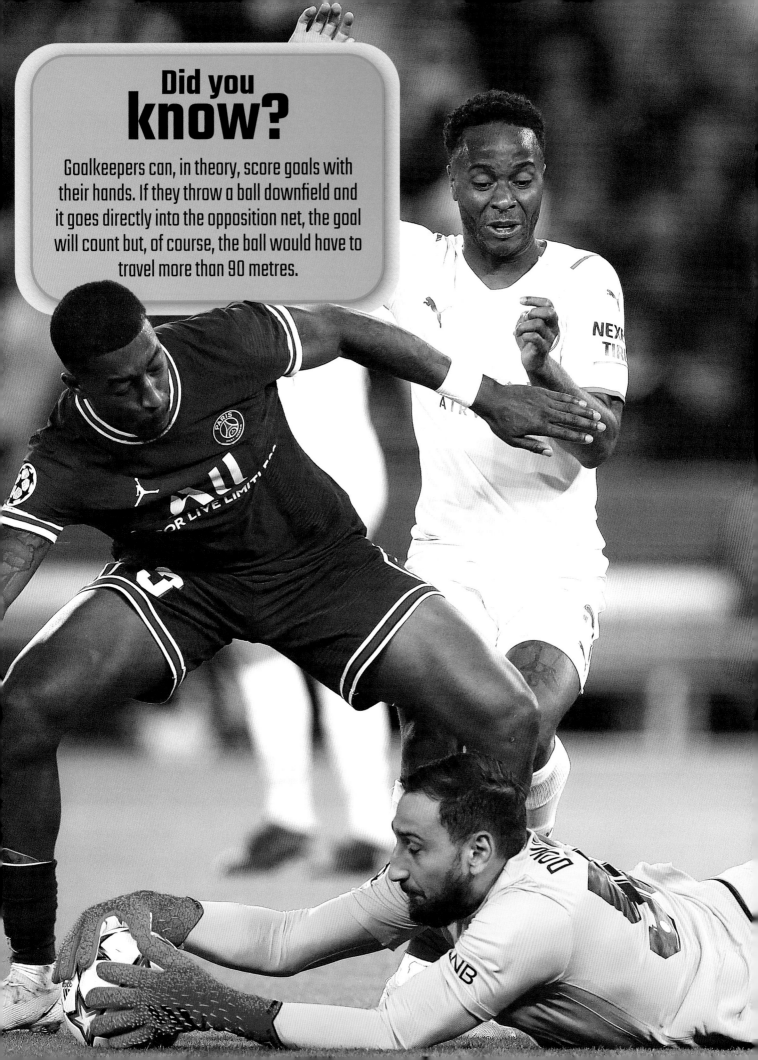

Did you **know?**

Goalkeepers can, in theory, score goals with their hands. If they throw a ball downfield and it goes directly into the opposition net, the goal will count but, of course, the ball would have to travel more than 90 metres.

1

NATIONALITY
Brazilian

CURRENT CLUB
Liverpool

ALISSON

The Brazilian has proved to be a top keeper at Liverpool. Alisson is a superb shot-stopper and great at dealing with crosses. Incredibly quick off his line to foil any threat, he can turn defence into attack by finding team-mates with long or short passes.

BIRTHDATE	02/10/1992
POSITION	GOALKEEPER
HEIGHT	1.91 M
WEIGHT	91 KG
PREFERRED FOOT	RIGHT

GOALS CONCEDED
186

APPEARANCES
222

PENALTIES SAVED
3

SAVES
568

CLEAN SHEETS
101

PENALTIES FACED
15

PUNCHES
90

CATCHES
86

MAJOR CLUB HONOURS
⚽ Premier League: 2020
⚽ UEFA Champions League: 2019
⚽ FIFA Club World Cup: 2019

INTERNATIONAL HONOURS
⚽ Copa América: 2019, runner-up 2021

ACTIVITY AREAS

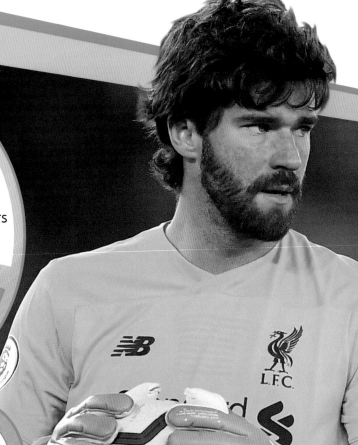

BONO

Bono (Yassine Bounou) was born in Canada but represents Morocco, the country where he grew up. Very brave and quick to assess dangerous situations, he cuts down angles very well, is an outstanding shot-stopper and also a great communicator.

BIRTHDATE	05/04/1991
POSITION	GOALKEEPER
HEIGHT	1.92 M
WEIGHT	78 KG
PREFERRED FOOT	RIGHT

GOALS CONCEDED 157

APPEARANCES 151

PENALTIES SAVED 4

CLEAN SHEETS 58

SAVES 443

PENALTIES FACED 30

CATCHES 69

PUNCHES 59

MAJOR CLUB HONOURS
⚽ UEFA Europa League: 2020

INTERNATIONAL HONOURS
⚽ None to date

ACTIVITY AREAS

1

THIBAUT COURTOIS

Thibaut Courtois uses his height to dominate his penalty area, catching crosses and punching well. An agile shot-stopper, he can get down low to make saves, communicates well with his defence, is excellent coming off his line and passes well.

BIRTHDATE	11/05/1992
POSITION	GOALKEEPER
HEIGHT	1.99 M
WEIGHT	96 KG
PREFERRED FOOT	LEFT

GOALS CONCEDED
403

APPEARANCES
442

PENALTIES SAVED
6

CLEAN SHEETS
188

SAVES
1074

PENALTIES FACED
38

PUNCHES
131

CATCHES
460

MAJOR CLUB HONOURS

⚽ La Liga: 2014 (Atlético Madrid), 2020 ⚽ Premier League: 2015, 2017 (Chelsea) ⚽ UEFA Europa League: 2012 (Atlético Madrid) ⚽ FIFA Club World Cup: 2018 ⚽ UEFA Super Cup: 2012 (Atlético Madrid)

INTERNATIONAL HONOURS

⚽ FIFA World Cup: third place 2018

ACTIVITY AREAS

DAVID DE GEA

David De Gea is an effective keeper, though unorthodox at times (he is known for using his legs to make saves). Agile and athletic, he marshals his penalty area well. His catching has improved, but he is still happier punching the ball the clear.

NATIONALITY
Spanish

CURRENT CLUB
Manchester United

BIRTHDATE	07/11/1990
POSITION	GOALKEEPER
HEIGHT	1.92 M
WEIGHT	76 KG
PREFERRED FOOT	RIGHT

GOALS CONCEDED
567

APPEARANCES
511

PENALTIES SAVED
8

CLEAN SHEETS
168

SAVES
1505

CATCHES
333

PENALTIES FACED
52

PUNCHES
167

MAJOR CLUB HONOURS
⚽ Premier League: 2013 ⚽ UEFA Europa League: 2010 (Atlético Madrid), 2017, runner-up 2021 ⚽ UEFA Super Cup: 2010 (Atlético Madrid) ⚽ FA Cup: 2016

INTERNATIONAL HONOURS
⚽ UEFA Nations League: runner-up 2021

ACTIVITY AREAS

PRIMEBLUE

NATIONALITY
Italian

CURRENT CLUB
Paris Saint-Germain

50

GIANLUIGI DONNARUMMA

The Italian is an amazing talent who made his Serie A debut aged just 16, won his first Italian cap at 17 and became a European champion at 22. Mentally strong and composed under pressure, he has everything it takes to become an all-time great.

BIRTHDATE	25/02/1999
POSITION	GOALKEEPER
HEIGHT	1.96 M
WEIGHT	90 KG
PREFERRED FOOT	RIGHT

GOALS CONCEDED
267

APPEARANCES
250

PENALTIES SAVED
9

CLEAN SHEETS
80

SAVES
715

PENALTIES FACED
39

CATCHES
159

PUNCHES
127

MAJOR CLUB HONOURS
- Supercoppa Italiana: 2016 (AC Milan)

INTERNATIONAL HONOURS
- UEFA European Championship: 2020
- UEFA Nations League: third place 2021

ACTIVITY AREAS

EDERSON

Owing to his range of passing and great ball skills, Ederson is often considered a playmaker goalkeeper and counted as one of the best in the English Premier League. He is a fine shot-stopper with a reputation for being a great penalty-kick saver, too.

NATIONALITY
Brazilian

CURRENT CLUB
Manchester City

31

BIRTHDATE	17/08/1993
POSITION	GOALKEEPER
HEIGHT	1.88 M
WEIGHT	86 KG
PREFERRED FOOT	LEFT

GOALS CONCEDED
185

APPEARANCES
234

PENALTIES SAVED
6

SAVES
440

CLEAN SHEETS
109

PENALTIES FACED
28

PUNCHES
58

CATCHES
106

MAJOR CLUB HONOURS
⚽ UEFA Champions League: runner-up 2021
⚽ Premier League: 2018, 2019, 2021
⚽ FA Cup: 2019

INTERNATIONAL HONOURS
⚽ Copa América: 2019, runner-up 2021

ACTIVITY AREAS

91

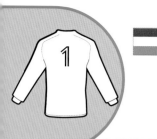

1

NATIONALITY
Hungarian

CURRENT CLUB
RB Leipzig

PÉTER GULÁCSI

Péter Gulácsi is dedicated to preparing for every football situation he faces. He studies approaching forwards to get an instinct for where they are going to shoot, gets into the right position and then makes difficult saves look very easy.

BIRTHDATE	06/05/1990
POSITION	GOALKEEPER
HEIGHT	1.91 M
WEIGHT	86 KG
PREFERRED FOOT	RIGHT

GOALS CONCEDED
295

APPEARANCES
247

PENALTIES SAVED
3

CLEAN SHEETS
73

SAVES
597

PENALTIES FACED
34

CATCHES
149

PUNCHES
67

MAJOR CLUB HONOURS
- Austrian Bundesliga: 2014, 2015 (Red Bull Salzburg)
- Austrian Cup: 2014, 2015 (Red Bull Salzburg)

INTERNATIONAL HONOURS
- FIFA U-20 World Cup: third place 2009

ACTIVITY AREAS

SAMIR HANDANOVIĆ

Samir Handanović has awesome positional sense, reaction time, agility, anticipation and athleticism — a combination that makes him an expert between the sticks. He is also a good communicator and defensive organiser.

 **NATIONALITY**
Slovenian

CURRENT CLUB
Internazionale

BIRTHDATE	14/07/1984
POSITION	GOALKEEPER
HEIGHT	1.93 M
WEIGHT	92 KG
PREFERRED FOOT	RIGHT

GOALS CONCEDED
672

APPEARANCES
616

PENALTIES SAVED
30

CLEAN SHEETS
217

SAVES
1796

PENALTIES FACED
94

CATCHES
578

PUNCHES
294

MAJOR CLUB HONOURS
⚽ Serie A: 2021

INTERNATIONAL HONOURS
⚽ None to date

ACTIVITY AREAS

1

NATIONALITY
French

CURRENT CLUB
Tottenham Hotspur

HUGO LLORIS

Hugo Lloris is a natural leader, good at organising his defence. Armed with excellent reflexes, he is brilliant at coming off his line to clear the danger and then distributing the ball quickly, which has earned him the sweeper-keeper label.

BIRTHDATE	26/12/1986
POSITION	GOALKEEPER
HEIGHT	1.88 M
WEIGHT	82 KG
PREFERRED FOOT	LEFT

GOALS CONCEDED
694

APPEARANCES
643

PENALTIES SAVED
10

SAVES
1795

CLEAN SHEETS
218

PENALTIES FACED
72

CATCHES
779

PUNCHES
400

MAJOR CLUB HONOURS
⚽ UEFA Champions League: runner-up 2019
⚽ Coupe de France: 2012 (Olympique Lyonnais)

INTERNATIONAL HONOURS
⚽ FIFA World Cup: 2018
⚽ UEFA Nations League: 2021
⚽ UEFA European Championship: runner-up 2016

ACTIVITY AREAS

94

EMILIANO MARTÍNEZ

An immensely athletic goalkeeper, Emiliano Martínez is capable of reaching shots going into the top corner with either hand. His quick feet mean he gets into good positions not only to make saves but also reduce the angle for shots.

NATIONALITY
Argentinian

CURRENT CLUB
Aston Villa

BIRTHDATE	02/09/1992
POSITION	GOALKEEPER
HEIGHT	1.95 M
WEIGHT	85 KG
PREFERRED FOOT	RIGHT

GOALS CONCEDED
120

APPEARANCES
97

PENALTIES SAVED
2

SAVES
299

CLEAN SHEETS
36

PENALTIES FACED
14

PUNCHES
14

CATCHES
93

MAJOR CLUB HONOURS
⚽ FA Cup: 2020 (Arsenal)

INTERNATIONAL HONOURS
⚽ Copa América: 2021

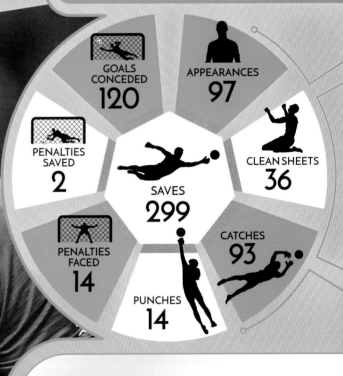

ACTIVITY AREAS

95

16

NATIONALITY
Senegalese

CURRENT CLUB
Chelsea

ÉDOUARD MENDY

French-born Édouard Mendy chose to play for his mother's birthplace Senegal. He is a great shot stopper who dominates his penalty area, marshals his defence and deals with aerial threats with supreme confidence.

BIRTHDATE	01/03/1992
POSITION	GOALKEEPER
HEIGHT	1.97 M
WEIGHT	86 KG
PREFERRED FOOT	RIGHT

GOALS CONCEDED
122

APPEARANCES
144

PENALTIES SAVED
2

CLEAN SHEETS
65

SAVES
336

PENALTIES FACED
21

CATCHES
95

PUNCHES
38

MAJOR CLUB HONOURS
- ⚽ UEFA Champions League: 2021
- ⚽ UEFA Super Cup: 2021
- ⚽ FIFA Club World Cup: 2021

INTERNATIONAL HONOURS
- ⚽ CAF Africa Cup of Nations: 2021, runner-up 2019

ACTIVITY AREAS

KEYLOR NAVAS

After fantastic performances at the 2014 FIFA World Cup, Keylor Navas earned a move to Europe and has since shown his quality and confidence at top-club level. He is an amazing shot-stopper, very agile, strong and great at dealing with crosses.

NATIONALITY
Costa Rican

CURRENT CLUB
Paris Saint-Germain

1

BIRTHDATE	15/12/1986
POSITION	GOALKEEPER
HEIGHT	1.85 M
WEIGHT	80 KG
PREFERRED FOOT	RIGHT

GOALS CONCEDED
269

APPEARANCES
291

PENALTIES SAVED
10

CLEAN SHEETS
110

SAVES
892

PENALTIES FACED
37

CATCHES
149

PUNCHES
119

MAJOR CLUB HONOURS
⚽ Ligue 1: 2020 ⚽ La Liga: 2017 (R. Mad.) ⚽ UEFA Champions League: 2016-18 (R. Mad.), runner-up 2020
⚽ FIFA Club World Cup: 2014, 2016-18 (R. Mad.) ⚽ UEFA Super Cup: 2014, 2016-17 (R. Mad.)

INTERNATIONAL HONOURS
⚽ None to date

ACTIVITY AREAS

97

1

NATIONALITY
German

CURRENT CLUB
Bayern Munich

MANUEL NEUER

Manuel Neuer is famous for being football's first sweeper-keeper. He is a fine shot-stopper who commands his penalty area and marshals the defence well. He is also great with the ball at his feet, allowing defenders to play further upfield.

BIRTHDATE	27/03/1986
POSITION	GOALKEEPER
HEIGHT	1.93 M
WEIGHT	92 KG
PREFERRED FOOT	RIGHT

GOALS CONCEDED
503

APPEARANCES
594

PENALTIES SAVED
11

CLEAN SHEETS
262

SAVES
1478

PENALTIES FACED
40

CATCHES
597

PUNCHES
265

MAJOR CLUB HONOURS

⚽ Bundesliga: 2013, 2014, 2015, 2016, 2017, 2018, 2019, 2020, 2021 ⚽ UEFA Champs League: 2013, 2020 ⚽ UEFA Super Cup: 2013, 2020 ⚽ FIFA Club World Cup: 2013, 2020 ⚽ DFB Pokal: 2011 (Schalke 04) 2013-14, 2016, 2019-20

INTERNATIONAL HONOURS

⚽ FIFA World Cup: 2014

ACTIVITY AREAS

JAN OBLAK

One of the world's most accomplished keepers, Jan Oblak is blessed with quick reflexes and agility, and he's excellent at coming off his line and organising his defence. His communication skills make him a reliable team vice-captain.

NATIONALITY
Slovenian

CURRENT CLUB
Atlético Madrid

13

BIRTHDATE	07/01/1993
POSITION	GOALKEEPER
HEIGHT	1.88 M
WEIGHT	87 KG
PREFERRED FOOT	RIGHT

GOALS CONCEDED
251

APPEARANCES
338

PENALTIES SAVED
9

SAVES
841

CLEAN SHEETS
168

PENALTIES FACED
37

PUNCHES
94

CATCHES
194

MAJOR CLUB HONOURS
- ⚽ La Liga: 2021
- ⚽ UEFA Champions League: runner-up 2016
- ⚽ UEFA Europa League: 2018
- ⚽ UEFA Super Cup: 2018

INTERNATIONAL HONOURS
- ⚽ None to date

ACTIVITY AREAS

25

NATIONALITY
Colombian

CURRENT CLUB
Napoli

DAVID OSPINA

David Ospina is strong in all areas of goalkeeping. He is an excellent shot stopper and always decisive when dealing with crosses. His tremendous agility and speed off the line makes him as effective as other taller goalkeepers.

BIRTHDATE	31/08/1988
POSITION	GOALKEEPER
HEIGHT	1.83 M
WEIGHT	76 KG
PREFERRED FOOT	RIGHT

GOALS CONCEDED
371

APPEARANCES
332

PENALTIES SAVED
7

CLEAN SHEETS
109

SAVES
970

PENALTIES FACED
39

CATCHES
458

PUNCHES
188

MAJOR CLUB HONOURS
⚽ Coppa Italia: 2020
⚽ FA Cup: 2015, 2017 (Arsenal)

INTERNATIONAL HONOURS
⚽ Copa América: third place 2016, 2021

ACTIVITY AREAS

KASPER SCHMEICHEL

NATIONALITY
Danish

CURRENT CLUB
Leicester City

1

Kasper Schmeichel, the son of the legendary keeper Peter Schmeichel, has many of his father's strengths. He is mentally strong and brilliant in one-on-one situations. He is also superb in the air, commands his penalty area and is a great ball distributor.

BIRTHDATE	05/11/1986
POSITION	GOALKEEPER
HEIGHT	1.89 M
WEIGHT	89 KG
PREFERRED FOOT	RIGHT

GOALS CONCEDED
388

APPEARANCES
302

PENALTIES SAVED
10

SAVES
849

CLEAN SHEETS
90

PENALTIES FACED
45

PUNCHES
128

CATCHES
201

MAJOR CLUB HONOURS
- ⚽ Premier League: 2016
- ⚽ FA Cup: 2021

INTERNATIONAL HONOURS
- ⚽ None to date

ACTIVITY AREAS

NATIONALITY
Polish

CURRENT CLUB
Juventus

WOJCIECH SZCZĘSNY

Wojciech Szczęsny has grown into one of Europe's top-class keepers. A natural shot-stopper with lightning reflexes, he is also great at controlling his penalty area, dealing with crosses and setting up counter-attacks with quick clearances.

BIRTHDATE	18/04/1990
POSITION	GOALKEEPER
HEIGHT	1.95 M
WEIGHT	90 KG
PREFERRED FOOT	RIGHT

GOALS CONCEDED
422

APPEARANCES
401

PENALTIES SAVED
15

CLEAN SHEETS
141

SAVES
1062

PENALTIES FACED
68

CATCHES
347

PUNCHES
167

MAJOR CLUB HONOURS
⚽ Serie A: 2018, 2019, 2020
⚽ FA Cup: 2014, 2015 (Arsenal)
⚽ Coppa Italia: 2018, 2021, runner-up 2020

INTERNATIONAL HONOURS
⚽ None to date

ACTIVITY AREAS

MARC-ANDRÉ TER STEGEN

NATIONALITY
German

CURRENT CLUB
Barcelona

A brilliant sweeper-keeper, Marc-André ter Stegen is simply world class. In addition to his fine goalkeeping qualities, he is exceptional at anticipating opponents who have beaten the offside trap, and can rush off his line to meet the danger.

BIRTHDATE	30/04/1992
POSITION	GOALKEEPER
HEIGHT	1.87 M
WEIGHT	85 KG
PREFERRED FOOT	RIGHT

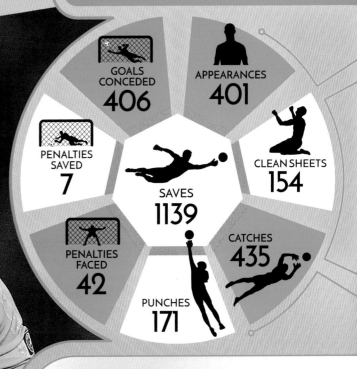

GOALS CONCEDED
406

APPEARANCES
401

PENALTIES SAVED
7

SAVES
1139

CLEAN SHEETS
154

PENALTIES FACED
42

PUNCHES
171

CATCHES
435

MAJOR CLUB HONOURS
⚽ La Liga: 2015, 2016, 2018, 2019 ⚽ UEFA Champions League: 2015 ⚽ UEFA Super Cup: 2015 ⚽ FIFA Club World Cup: 2015 ⚽ Copa del Rey: 2015, 2016, 2017, 2018, 2021

INTERNATIONAL HONOURS
⚽ FIFA Confederations Cup: 2017

ACTIVITY AREAS

MANAGERS

Head coaches are as different to each other as players who play in different positions. But the majority of the 12 featured in this section have one thing in common: they are all winners, either in their domestic leagues or in continental competitions. Some, such as Diego Simeone, were legendary players in their own right and title winners well before they entered management, while others, such as Liverpool boss Jürgen Klopp, did little on the field but have had great success as the brains behind a top side.

WHAT DO THE STATS MEAN?

GAMES MANAGED
This is the number of matches the coach has been in charge of across their career in top-flight football.

TEAMS MANAGED
The number of clubs (first teams only) that the coach has managed during their career to date.

WINS
This is the number of games the coach has won, including one leg of a cup-tie, even if the tie was lost on aggregate or penalties.

TROPHIES
The trophy list features the head coach's success in domestic top divisions, national and league cups and international club competitions, except any super cups.

Did you know?

Chelsea coach Thomas Tuchel looks at the psychological elements that underpin a player's performance. At Mainz he subjected his players to a mental test which yielded a 30-page evaluation of each squad member.

CARLO ANCELOTTI

Formerly an international player, Carlo Ancelotti uses different systems depending on the opposition and players available. His favourite formation is 4–4–2, sometimes in a diamond, other times with four midfielders in a line across the pitch.

NATIONALITY
Italian

CURRENT CLUB
Real Madrid

YEARS AS HEAD COACH: 27

FIRST CLUB: REGGIANA

CLUBS MANAGED	GAMES	LEAGUE TITLES
10	1216	4

WINS	DRAW	LOSSES
709	278	229

CHAMPIONS LEAGUE TROPHIES	EUROPA LEAGUE TROPHIES	OTHER TROPHIES*
3	0	6

MAJOR CLUB HONOURS

- ⚽ UEFA Champions League: 2003, 2007 (Milan), 2014 (R. Madrid)
- ⚽ FIFA Club World Cup: 2007 (AC Milan), 2014 (R. Madrid)
- ⚽ UEFA Super Cup: 1993, 2007 (Milan), 2014 (R. Madrid)
- ⚽ UEFA Intertoto Cup: 1999 (Juventus)
- ⚽ Serie A: 2004 (AC Milan)
- ⚽ Premier League: 2010 (Chelsea)
- ⚽ Ligue 1: 2013 (Paris St Germain)
- ⚽ Copa del Rey: 2014 (Real Madrid)
- ⚽ Bundesliga: 2017 (Bayern Munich)

*Excludes Super Cups

ANTONIO CONTE

Although Antonio Conte varies his tactics and formations, they are always based on a strong defence, so his teams tend to be great counter-attackers. Always animated on the touchline, he instils a great team spirit into his side.

NATIONALITY
Italian

CURRENT CLUB
Tottenham Hotspur

YEARS AS HEAD COACH : 16

FIRST CLUB: AREZZO

CLUBS MANAGED	GAMES	LEAGUE TITLES
9	565	5

WINS	DRAW	LOSSES
332	134	99

CHAMPIONS LEAGUE TROPHIES	EUROPA LEAGUE TROPHIES	OTHER TROPHIES*
0	0	1

MAJOR CLUB HONOURS

- ⚽ Serie A: 2012, 2013, 2014 (Juventus), 2021 (Internazionale)
- ⚽ Premier League: 2017 (Chelsea)
- ⚽ FA Cup: 2018 (Chelsea)
- ⚽ UEFA Europa League: runner-up 2020 (Internazionale)

*Excludes Super Cups

UNAI EMERY

Unai Emery has enjoyed great success managing clubs that have a modest budget. His preference is a 4–2–3–1 formation or 4–4–2 — the choice dependant on the attacking skills of two central midfielders and their ability to retain possession.

NATIONALITY
Spanish

CURRENT CLUB
Villareal

YEARS AS HEAD COACH: 18

FIRST CLUB: LORCA DEPORTIVA

CLUBS MANAGED	GAMES	LEAGUE TITLES
8	899	1

WINS	DRAW	LOSSES
478	201	220

CHAMPIONS LEAGUE TROPHIES	EUROPA LEAGUE TROPHIES	OTHER TROPHIES*
1	4	4

*Excludes Super Cups

MAJOR CLUB HONOURS
- ⚽ UEFA Europa League: 2014, 2015, 2016 (Sevilla), 2021, runner-up 2019 (Arsenal)
- ⚽ Ligue 1: 2018 (Paris Saint-Germain)
- ⚽ Coupe de France: 2017, 2018 (Paris Saint-Germain)

PEP GUARDIOLA

Once a great midfielder himself, Pep Guardiola devised the *tika-taka* passing system at Barcelona (2008–12). Disciplined in possession, without the ball his teams press the opposition into making mistakes and then launch rapid counter-attacks.

NATIONALITY
Spanish

CURRENT CLUB
Manchester City

YEARS AS HEAD COACH: 18

FIRST CLUB: BARCELONA

CLUBS MANAGED	GAMES	LEAGUE TITLES
3	791	9

WINS	DRAW	LOSSES
577	120	94

CHAMPIONS LEAGUE TROPHIES	EUROPA LEAGUE TROPHIES	OTHER TROPHIES*
2	0	12

*Excludes Super Cups

MAJOR CLUB HONOURS
- ⚽ UEFA Champions League: 2009, 2011 (Barcelona), runner-up 2021
- ⚽ UEFA Super Cup: 2009, 2011 (Barcelona), 2013 (B. Munich)
- ⚽ FIFA Club World Cup: 2009, 2011 (Barcelona), 2013 (B. Munich)
- ⚽ La Liga: 2009, 2010, 2011 (Barcelona)
- ⚽ Bundesliga: 2014, 2015, 2016 (B. Munich)
- ⚽ Premier League: 2018, 2019, 2021
- ⚽ FA Cup: 2019

JÜRGEN KLOPP

Jürgen Klopp brings great enthusiasm to the technical area and expects his team to show a similar spirit. His team are strong defensively, try to win back the ball immediately after they lose it and counter-attack at great speed.

NATIONALITY
German

CURRENT CLUB
Liverpool

YEARS AS HEAD COACH:	21
FIRST CLUB:	MAINZ 05

CLUBS MANAGED	GAMES	LEAGUE TITLES
3	955	3

WINS	DRAW	LOSSES
512	230	213

CHAMPIONS LEAGUE TROPHIES	EUROPA LEAGUE TROPHIES	OTHER TROPHIES*
1	0	3

MAJOR CLUB HONOURS
- ⚽ UEFA Champions League: 2019, runner-up 2013 (Borussia Dortmund), 2018
- ⚽ UEFA Super Cup: 2019
- ⚽ FIFA Club World Cup: 2019
- ⚽ Bundesliga: 2011, 2012 (Borussia Dortmund)
- ⚽ DFB-Pokal: 2012 (Borussia Dortmund)
- ⚽ Premier League: 2020
- ⚽ EFL Cup: 2022

*Excludes Super Cups

JULEN LOPETEGUI

Julen Lopetegui likes his teams to be creative in attack and wants his full-backs to give width, dragging defenders out of position and then filling the gaps they leave behind. He preaches a never give up attitude from his teams.

NATIONALITY
Spanish

CURRENT CLUB
Sevilla

YEARS AS HEAD COACH:	19
FIRST CLUB:	RAYO VALLECANO

CLUBS MANAGED	GAMES	LEAGUE TITLES
5	276	0

WINS	DRAW	LOSSES
161	64	51

CHAMPIONS LEAGUE TROPHIES	EUROPA LEAGUE TROPHIES	OTHER TROPHIES*
0	1	0

MAJOR CLUB HONOURS
- ⚽ UEFA Europa League: 2020
- ⚽ UEFA Super Cup: runner-up 2020
- ⚽ UEFA Super Cup: runner-up 2018 (Real Madrid)

*Excludes Super Cups

JOSÉ MOURINHO

José Mourinho focuses his team strength on midfield, normally with a player in front of the defence and two or three further upfield. He expects his defenders to be tactically and technically excellent, and tends to pick experienced players.

NATIONALITY
Portuguese

CURRENT CLUB
AS Roma

YEARS AS HEAD COACH: 22

FIRST CLUB: BENFICA

CLUBS MANAGED	GAMES	LEAGUE TITLES
9	1040	8

WINS	DRAW	LOSSES
658	213	169

CHAMPIONS LEAGUE TROPHIES	EUROPA LEAGUE TROPHIES	OTHER TROPHIES*
2	2	8

MAJOR CLUB HONOURS
- ⚽ UEFA Champions League: 2004 (Porto), 2010 (Inter Milan)
- ⚽ UEFA Europa League: 2017 (Manchester United)
- ⚽ UEFA Cup: 2003 (Porto)
- ⚽ Premier League: 2005, 2006, 2015 (Chelsea)
- ⚽ FA Cup: 2007 (Chelsea)
- ⚽ Serie A: 2009, 2010 (Inter Milan)
- ⚽ Coppa Italia: 2010 (Inter Milan)
- ⚽ La Liga: 2012 (Real Madrid)
- ⚽ Copa del Rey: 2011 (Real Madrid)

*Excludes Super Cups

JULIAN NAGELSMANN

Julian Nagelsmann retired from playing aged 24 and moved into coaching while studying sports science at university. He is great at match preparation and is happy to get his teams to change formation with or without possession of the ball.

NATIONALITY
German

CURRENT CLUB
Bayern Munich

YEARS AS HEAD COACH: 6

FIRST CLUB: 1899 HOFFENHEIM

CLUBS MANAGED	GAMES	LEAGUE TITLES
3	272	0

WINS	DRAW	LOSSES
140	69	63

CHAMPIONS LEAGUE TROPHIES	EUROPA LEAGUE TROPHIES	OTHER TROPHIES*
0	0	0

MAJOR CLUB HONOURS
- ⚽ DFB-Pokal: runner-up 2021 (RB Leipzig)

*Excludes Super Cups

MAURICIO POCHETTINO

NATIONALITY
Argentinian

Mauricio Pochettino made his reputation at Barcelona's second club Espanyol before coming to England. His teams play open football, featuring technically good defenders, a spearhead striker and midfielders attacking from deeper positions.

CURRENT CLUB
Paris Saint-Germain

| YEARS AS HEAD COACH: | 13 |
| FIRST CLUB: | ESPANYOL |

CLUBS MANAGED	GAMES	LEAGUE TITLES
4	591	0

WINS	DRAW	LOSSES
286	130	175

CHAMPIONS LEAGUE TROPHIES	EUROPA LEAGUE TROPHIES	OTHER TROPHIES*
0	0	1

*Excludes Super Cups

MAJOR CLUB HONOURS
- UEFA Champions League runner-up 2019 (Tottenham Hotspur)
- Coupe de France: 2021

STEFANO PIOLI

NATIONALITY
Italian

Stefano Pioli is superb at instilling confidence into his players. This is partly because he is flexible with his tactics and focuses more on the management of the individuals, getting the best out of them on the pitch. He favours a 4–2–3–1 formation.

CURRENT CLUB
AC Milan

| YEARS AS HEAD COACH: | 25 |
| FIRST CLUB: | SALERNITANA |

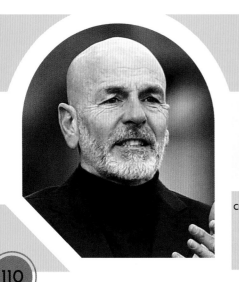

CLUBS MANAGED	GAMES	LEAGUE TITLES
14	760	0

WINS	DRAW	LOSSES
305	226	229

CHAMPIONS LEAGUE TROPHIES	EUROPA LEAGUE TROPHIES	OTHER TROPHIES*
0	0	0

*Excludes Super Cups

MAJOR CLUB HONOURS
- None to date

DIEGO SIMEONE

Diego Simeone likes to use a formation which is almost a 4–2–2–2 unit, with wide midfielders playing between the two central ones and the strikers. Strong defensively, his teams are great at defending set pieces and dangerous in attack.

NATIONALITY
Argentinian

CURRENT CLUB
Atlético Madrid

YEARA AS HEAD COACH: 16

FIRST CLUB: RACING CLUB

CLUBS MANAGED	GAMES	LEAGUE TITLES
6	777	4

WINS	DRAW	LOSSES
433	185	159

CHAMPIONS LEAGUE TROPHIES	EUROPA LEAGUE TROPHIES	OTHER TROPHIES*
0	2	1

*Excludes Super Cups

MAJOR CLUB HONOURS
- ⚽ UEFA Champions League: runner-up 2014, 2016
- ⚽ UEFA Europa League: 2012, 2018
- ⚽ UEFA Super Cup: 2012, 2018
- ⚽ La Liga: 2014, 2021
- ⚽ Copa del Rey: 2013
- ⚽ Primera División Apertura 2006 (Estudiantes)
- ⚽ Primera División Clausura 2008 (Racing Club)

THOMAS TUCHEL

Thomas Tuchel has won multiple trophies. He is flexible, changing tactics to suit the players he has available, and a strong believer in *Gegenpressing*, immediately trying to regain possession rather than dropping into a more defensive mode.

NATIONALITY
German

CURRENT CLUB
Chelsea

YEARS AS HEAD COACH: 15

FIRST CLUB: MAINZ 05

CLUBS MANAGED	GAMES	LEAGUE TITLES
4	499	2

WINS	DRAW	LOSSES
285	101	113

CHAMPIONS LEAGUE TROPHIES	EUROPA LEAGUE TROPHIES	OTHER TROPHIES*
1	0	4

*Excludes Super Cups

MAJOR CLUB HONOURS
- ⚽ UEFA Champions League: 2021, runner-up 2020 (Paris Saint-Germain)
- ⚽ FIFA World Club Cup: 2021
- ⚽ UEFA Super Cup: 2021
- ⚽ Ligue 1: 2019, 2020 (Paris Saint-Germain)
- ⚽ Coupe de France: 2020 (Paris Saint-Germain)
- ⚽ DfB Pokal: 2017 (Borussia Dortmund)
- ⚽ Coupe de la Ligue: 2020 (PSG)

NOTES